Order and Ministry

Order and Ministry

edited by
Christine Hall
and
Robert Hannaford

Gracewing.

First published in 1996

Gracewing
Fowler Wright Books
2 Southern Ave, Leominster
Herefordshire, HR6 0QF

The right of the editors and contributors to be identified as
the authors of this work has been asserted in accordance with
the Copyright, Designs and Patents Act 1988.

ISBN 0 85244 279 3

Typesetting by Reesprint
Radley, Oxfordshire, OX14 3AJ

Printed by Redwood Books
Trowbridge, Wiltshire, BA14 8RN

Contents

Notes on Contributors

Brian Capper is Senior Lecturer in Religious Studies, Canterbury Christ Church College.

Peter Davie is Senior Lecturer in Religious Studies, Canterbury Christ Church College, and honorary assistant priest to Canterbury City Centre Parish.

Christine Hall is Director of the Bishop Otter Centre for Theology and Ministry, and Senior Lecturer in Theology and Ministry, Chichester Institute, and a diocesan deacon in the Diocese of Chichester.

John Halliburton is Chancellor and Canon Residentiary of St Paul's Cathedral, London.

Robert Hannaford is Senior Lecturer in Religious Studies, Canterbury Christ Church College.

Brian Horne is Senior Lecturer in Christian Doctrine, King's College, London.

Geoffrey Rowell is Bishop of Basingstoke.

H.J.M. Turner is an author and translator, and former college educator. In retirement, he is honorary assistant curate at St Botolph-without-Bishopsgate, London.

Foreword

Christine Hall

A word of explanation is perhaps necessary to enable readers of *Order And Ministry* to understand how and why it came to take shape.

In *Faith in Momentum*, published in 1990, George Guiver set out to show 'in however inadequate a way it may be, that the Church, in many facets of its life, though not in all, is reduced to living off mere shavings of something greater, a reality which is its true birthright'.[1] At the time when Guiver was writing, some of us were working closely together on *The Deacon's Ministry*.[2] We were in a position to feel the full force of his words, as we were gradually discovering, somewhat to our surprise, the vital significance of the order of deacon. Historically, theologically and in relation to contemporary needs, we were beginning to see the greater tree on which the 'mere shaving' had originated and from which it continued to take its origin and life, despite having been considered for many centuries a brief twelve-month halt on the way to priesthood.

The insights gained during research on the diaconate led to this present attempt to explore more fully the wider subjects of ministry and order, and their relation to each other. The diaconate, of all the orders of bishop, priest and deacon, quite clearly appeared, and doubtless still appears in much popular perception, as the most useless. From the contemporary functional perspective of ministry, the diaconate is often written off with the claim that a deacon 'can do nothing that anyone else cannot do'. As we contemplated the all-too-possible parody of a church in which priests existed because they had somehow clung to the exclusive right to consecrate the elements at the Eucharist, and bishops because they alone could confirm and ordain, it seemed to us that a number of questions could usefully be asked and a number of other possible scenarios described. Sadly, it seemed that much contemporary understanding of ministry and order, and the way bishops, deacons, priests and lay ministers relate to each other pastorally and liturgically, did indicate that this was an area where the Church was indeed 'reduced to living off mere shavings of something greater'. In the situation which presented itself, other words of George Guiver also rang true:

> Bits and pieces of Tradition are taken up and put to use, according largely to preference, and affectionately held on to in tandem with the individual pursuit of personal stances. It is interesting to see how often people and institutions which pride themselves on their critical and adventurous stance fall back at certain points on traditional items, such as vestments, ceremonies or the prizing of spiritual classics. But these are now fragments scattered like confetti in a fragmented community, whose ultimate source of authority is the autonomous individual, who is free to maintain a critical attitude towards the Church, a cautious embrace of an institution which is so prone to become absorbed in itself that any allegiance must be hedged about with conditions.
>
> The inevitable result is that Christians are not held together: they have not a Church with a gospel to proclaim, but a Church with a stalemate, a mere arena in which different people pursue their preferences.[3]

This volume has been put together by inviting a number of people, from different Anglican backgrounds and styles, to write about the aspects of order and ministry which seem to raise most questions at the present time. Brian Capper and John Halliburton examine the nature of ministry and order in the New Testament writings and in the early Church period, the latter going on to tell the story of the subsequent hijacking of ministry by the clergy and its concomitant effects. H.J.M. Turner discusses the nature of vocation, questioning the way it is understood and applied to ordained ministry in the contemporary Church. Brian Horne offers a trinitarian theology of order, which clearly and compellingly shows the relationship between the Church's outer forms of ministry and her inner and hidden life, whilst Robert Hannaford addresses a number of related questions on the theology of ministry as a whole, including a challenge to the Church's accepted limited understanding of *diakonia*. Peter Davie traces the functional idea of ordained ministry from the Reformation onwards in the Church of England, and Geoffrey Rowell draws the whole together in an Afterword. Readers will not find total consistency, for one contributor takes for granted points which are a matter of debate for another. Other avenues could have been explored: other writers' views could have been invited, or have indeed been given in other published works.

The questions the contributors address are not new or even particularly characteristic of the present day, though they are acutely felt by the Church of England as it grapples with the aftermath of the decision to ordain women to the priesthood and as it relates to other ecclesial bodies in ecumenical exchange and dialogue. Some fifty years ago, a volume of essays entitled *The Apostolic Ministry* was published under the editorship of the then Bishop of Oxford, Dr Kenneth Kirk.[4] In his Introduction to the first edition, Dr Kirk noted the contemporary desire for unity, and the conferences and discussions which had clarified many existing divisions. He then wrote:

> . . . it has become generally recognised that the crux of the whole matter is the doctrine of the ministry. Is the ministry from above or from below? Is it a gift to the Church from her Founder and Saviour, or an expedient evolved by the Church to meet the exigencies of her daily life? Has it a commission transmitted in orderly sequence from the Lord Himself or is it commissioned simply and solely by the congregation of believers among whom the minister is to serve? Clearly, here is a problem upon whose peaceful solution the future largely depends; it would be difficult for bodies holding diametrically

opposite views on such a matter to coalesce into a single harmonious or effective organisation.[5]

At the present time, the difficulty of holding together 'diametrically opposed views' is being widely experienced, and it is hoped that the publication of this volume will therefore prove timely. The Porvoo process[6] obliges participating Christian bodies to a re-examination of their ordained ministry, particularly episcopate and diaconate, in the context of a renewed understanding of the ministry of all the baptised. Lively debate is already in progress in the Nordic and Baltic Churches. Other ecumenical relationships in our day make similar demands on our grasp of the inter-relatedness of ministry and order.

Experience suggests we should agree that it is indeed 'difficult for bodies holding diametrically opposite views' on order and ministry 'to coalesce into a single and harmonious or effective organisation'. *Order and Ministry* is offered to the Church in the hope that it may contribute in some way to deeper and more harmonious understanding.

Notes

1. Guiver, G., *Faith in Momentum* (SPCK, 1990), p. 3.
2. Hall, C. (ed.), *The Deacon's Ministry* (Gracewing, 1991). This volume includes a contribution by Robert Hannaford, 'Towards a Theology of the Diaconate', to which readers should refer, if interested in a discussion about the relationship of the *diakonia* of the whole Church to the *diakonia* of those who belong to the order of deacon.
3. Guiver, op. cit., p. 66.
4. Kirk, K. (ed.), *The Apostolic Ministry* (Hodder and Stoughton repr. 1957). Subtitled *Essays on the History and Doctrine of Episcopacy*, this volume contains important work by a number of scholars on areas more widely relevant to order and ministry than the titles suggest.
5. Kirk, op. cit., p. xxi.
6. See *Together in Mission and Ministry: The Porvoo Common Statement with Essays on Church and Ministry in Northern Europe* (Church House Publishing, 1993).

1

The Republic, the Hierarchy, and the Trinity: A Theology of Order

Brian Horne

I

The collect for the Feast of St Michael and All Angels in the Book of Common Prayer serenely asks the worshipper to contemplate the marvellous ordering of the universe by the Creator: 'O Everlasting God, who hast ordained and constituted the services of Angels and men in a wonderful order; Mercifully grant, that as thy holy Angels alway do thee service in heaven, so by thy appointment they may succour and defend us on earth . . .' And modern sensibilities draw back, perplexed and unsure not merely because doubts arise about the existence of angelic beings and their ability to engage with the affairs of the material world, but because the concept of the ordered universe has itself become problematic. Similarly, when the preface of the old Ordinal of the Church of England begins with the assertion: 'It is evident unto all men diligently reading holy Scripture and Ancient Authors, that from the Apostles' time there have been these Orders of Ministers in Christ's Church: Bishops, Priests, and Deacons', we tend to shrink from such confidence, not merely because historical scholarship has cast doubt upon the security of the claim, but because the idea of order in the Church has become elusive, difficult to define and comprehend. In nearly every Christian community today a sense of unease is engendered when the concept of order is introduced into ecclesiological discussion. One feels one is treading on slippery and dangerous ground. There is a sense of confusion about what implications adherence to such a concept might have for the actual organisation of the Church, and an emotional ambivalence that is barely articulated but which informs, and often hinders, all attempts at achieving intellectual clarity. Consequently an apologetic tone enters the teaching and preaching of those churches which have inherited, and wish to maintain, a clearly recognised hierarchical structure. The word 'hierarchy' itself has become so laden with derogatory connotations that it cannot be used positively without elaborate and wearisome qualifications. To some extent this ambivalence towards the idea of order and the hostility towards that of hierarchy have been caused by the concepts' apparently inevitable association with a notion of authority which, itself, often induces a profound sense of disquiet in a community ostensibly dedicated to the preaching of a gospel of personal freedom. Of course, resistance to authority is not a new phenomenon in Christian history; nor is ambivalence to the establishment and maintenance of order a strange occurrence in Christian communities. The letters of St Paul provide us with ample evidence of such attitudes in the earliest churches, and the history of Christianity is littered with conflicts about authority and its exercise; but the present era demonstrates a peculiarly vivid sense of disquiet in this area of theology (and practice) which is only partly explained by the internal history of the Church. In a large measure our present ecclesiastical predicament has been caused by entirely non-ecclesiastical factors.

It cannot have escaped the notice of even the superficial observer of our society at this stage of its civility that the twin concepts of law and order are most frequently invoked by those whose political and social understanding of themselves and the world they inhabit is of the most conservative, even reactionary, kind. The need for the strict enforcement of law and order at the social and political levels is an idea assiduously propagated by them as the only defence against the onset of chaos, and is frequently, insidiously, identified with the interests of those who are already in possession of economic and political power. We thus witness the degeneration of concepts which have occupied central places in the political philosophy of Western European society and have been a formative influence on Judaeo-Christian culture. The once noble ideal of the Rule of Law comes to be perceived as an instrument of oppression, and the concept of the right ordering of society is seen as a principle which, at best, is concerned with the propping up of obsolete and meaningless structures and ceremonies, and, at worst, one which preserves and hallows existing privileges in such a way as to stultify the community, preventing the possibility of innovation, flexibility and growth.

In the last decade of the eighteenth century Edmund Burke reflected upon the revolution which had just taken place in France. While acknowledging the need for change in every society he argued that 'good order' was 'the foundation of all things'. 'Kings' he predicted, 'will be tyrants from policy, when subjects are rebels from principle'.[1] The remark was prescient, an indication of how deeply he understood the meaning of the recent events in France and how far-reaching their effects would be on European sensibility. Others, also seeing the French Revolution as some kind of watershed in European history, have developed this perception in different ways. Recently Jurgen Moltmann, for example, has put forward the theory that, since the French Revolution, European thinking has come to accept what he calls a 'historical' interpretation of reality. That is to say that a 'cosmological' orientation has given way, in the European mind, to an orientation that interprets reality as a state of constant and unstoppable change.

Since, with the French Revolution, 'revolution' *per se* has come to be understood as 'the distinctive mark of our era of world history' (F.J. Stahl), the church's orientation towards world history has become general, for 'history' is only a softer word for revolution, and historical experience is simply the experience of crisis.[2]

In fact, it would be possible to argue that the 'historical' or revolutionary reading of reality as opposed to the 'cosmological' reading had begun much earlier — at least two centuries before the French Revolution. The tension between the 'cosmological' and the 'historical' interpretations of both society and the individual had already become a dominant and disturbing theme of political and religious life in the sixteenth century. That most brilliant 'mirror of the age', William Shakespeare, invariably made this tension a central theme in nearly all of his 'history' plays, and used it as the philosophical axis of *Troilus and Cressida*. It will be useful to look at the presentation of the argument in this play, for it encapsulates the continuing conflict between different interpretations of reality. On the one hand stands the Greek encampment whose ideals are represented by Ulysses, who argues for the cosmological view in a famous speech on the necessity for order.

> The heavens themselves, the planets, and this centre
> Observe degree, priority, and place,
>
> . . . . .
>
> O! when degree is shak'd
> Which is the ladder to all high designs,
> The enterprise is sick.
>
> . . . . .
>
> Take but degree away, untune that string,
> And, hark! what discord follows; each thing meets
> In mere oppugnancy.   (Act I, Sc. III)

On the other hand there are the young warriors of the city of Troy who dismiss a world of fixed values and recognised status. The abduction of Helen, for purely personal motives, by Paris, is defended ardently by Troilus.

> . . . . Nay, if we talk of reason,
> Let's shut our gates and sleep: manhood and honour
> Should have hare-hearts, would they but fat their thoughts
> With this cramm'd reason: reason and respect
> Make livers pale, and lustihood deject.   (Act II, Sc. II)

It seems, at this point, no more than a young blood's romantic desire for flamboyant action, but, in response to Hector's sensible suggestion that the keeping of Helen is not worth the cost of the city of Troy, Troilus gives a reply that is, in effect, a refutation of Ulysses' discourse on order: 'What is aught, but as 'tis valued?' All given hierarchies are challenged by this question: the concept of order itself placed under a sceptical scrutiny. This challenge troubled the Tudor monarchs and eventually issued in a revolution that overturned both the Crown and the church in the seventeenth century. The French Revolution, perhaps, should be read as the practical 'achievement' of certain theories that had been occupying the European mind for more than two hundred years.

Troilus and Cressida probably appeared in the last decade of the sixteenth century, three decades after the Elizabethan Settlement had been promulgated. That Settlement can be seen as an attempt to construct an edifice which would preserve much of the medieval 'cosmological' interpretation of reality, in both church and State; and Richard Hooker writing in the last decades of that century (at the same time as Shakespeare's play) provided the Church of England with a majestic defence of the concept of order, perhaps the last of the great 'cosmological' interpretations of reality. In his Laws of Ecclesiastical Polity the whole universe is perceived as a vast and intricate system — an order — held in place by the laws of God. Natural and supernatural laws are part of a single continuum: the natural order is but the expression in the visible world of the supernatural order of the invisible universe. The ordering of both church and State are part of the providential workings of the divine Law Giver. If the 'string' of 'degree' is 'untuned' discord follows and 'each thing meets in mere oppugnancy'. The Church of England, like the Roman Catholic Church, has retained this interpretation of reality, usually unconsciously, as the philosophical foundation for the ordering of its sacred ministry up to the present day. This was not the view of the Puritans, nor of the most advanced (and increasingly sceptical) philosophers of the age. They made strange bedfellows, but together they succeeded in overturning the synthesis between church and State created by the Elizabethan Settlement; and, challenging the concept of order articulated by Hooker, they accomplished the revolution which ended with the execution of Charles I and the establishment of the Commonwealth.

It should be noted, however, that a protest against the cosmological interpretation of reality had already come from a different quarter seventy years before Hooker (and Shakespeare) in the figure of Martin Luther. In the treatises of 1520 Luther was already beginning to question the cosmological interpretation of reality and the significance of the external order of the Christian community. His was a revolutionary vision. He accepted the necessity of some form of church government and ecclesiastical order and, indeed, was prepared to use the traditional institutions, but not on the grounds that they conveyed a picture of the way reality should be understood. Unlike Calvin, or the Catholic Church, he attached no particular theological significance to them. The ordering of the church was to be a matter of convenience. All forms and structures were historically conditioned, variable, provisional and, in the end, dispensable. As such they offered no clue to the meaning of Christian life. God was to be encountered in His Word, and this encounter was an 'experience of crisis' (Moltmann); the perspective is individualistic and revolutionary. Any ecclesiastical order was subsequent to the initial personal encounter and was to be determined by the needs of the critical moment. It is the religious equivalent of 'What is aught but as 'tis valued?' Perhaps nowhere was Luther closer to the avant-garde theories of his secular contemporaries than in his revolutionary ecclesiology.

In the years since the Lutheran revolution in the sphere of the doctrine of the church, and the French Revolution in the sphere of practical politics, it would seem that the cosmological interpretation of reality commends itself to fewer and fewer people in religious and secular societies alike. It is inevitable that in this modern context troublesome and serious questions are thrust upon those who live within highly structured ecclesial communities. The contemporary political and religious world seems to favour change, novelty and fluidity. One extreme development of the historical interpretation of reality can be seen in the political doctrine of perpetual revolution, another is the phenomenon of post-modernism in which a basic tenet is actually the denial of any single interpretation of reality. In this latter case we can see that the historical interpretation has itself vanished in the plethora of competing and mutually contradictory world views. And what of the church and its order in all this? Can it continue to maintain a concept of order which is associated with a world view that is no longer accepted or even understood? Does one abandon the world view but try to re-define the idea of right order in another context? Or is it possible to expound a cosmological interpretation of reality that will be recognised once again as speaking to the human condition? Is it possible to find a way of interpreting reality that will reconcile the cosmological and historical understandings? I suggest that there is and that it might be called the sacramental interpretation. It will provide the epistemological undergirding of a theology of order.

As human beings inhabiting a material universe we are 'set in the order of signs'. Our lives are lived by, in and through complicated systems of signs. We make signs and are made by signs. We cannot escape this reality into a signless world. 'So far from signs (including language itself) being a regrettable necessity in view of our minds being muffled up in our bodies, they are intrinsic to our actual thinking and living as bodies.'[3] As complex creatures of matter and spirit we not only create sign-systems by which we communicate and express ourselves; we allow ourselves to be formed and shaped by the sign-systems we enter and embrace. But a sign, by definition, points away from itself; and a religious sign is one which points to a reality beyond the merely human but which, in and through the human, orders and re-orders our lives. Here the cosmological and the historical interpretations can be re-located. In this understanding of reality the Church itself is a sign: the sign of the Kingdom of God. And how can life in the Kingdom be described? In many ways, but the fundamental way will be in terms of the life of God Himself, for it is into that life that we are ultimately called. A theology of order will rest upon the doctrine of the Trinity.

II

One of the crucial interests of all human societies at all stages of their development has been that of the establishment of the proper relationship between the needs and interests of the individual and those of the group to which he or she belongs. It is the perennial theme of political philosophy, and different political systems offer different solutions to the problem. Where the importance of the collective is emphasised and the good of 'the whole' is the goal of political activity, the individual tends to be crushed, to be subsumed into the mass, and disappears. By contrast, where individual freedoms and rights are absolutised the result can be anarchy and the disappearance of society as such. What can be observed in political structures can also be seen in churches. The discovery of the proper relationship between the One and the Many is vital to the life of both 'polis' and Church. Moreover, if the Church is truly the company of those who have been redeemed, 'set free' by Christ, it is to be expected that in His Body the ideal relationship between the individual member and whole community must be manifest.

During the last few years writers on ecclesiological matters have turned their attention more and more to the notion of community and the essentially relational quality of human

existence; and no-one has been more concerned to demonstrate the truth of these propositions than the Greek Orthodox theologian, John Zizioulas. Over and over again he
returns, in his essays, to the question of personhood, to the
task of persuading his readers that true personhood is
achieved only in relationship. This looks like a stating of the
obvious until one realises how far the doctrine is pressed.
Personhood is seen, not as lying within the grasp of a discrete
interior identity: one becomes a person not by the possession
of individuality which is developed from within at will, not
by the assertion of some kind of individual essence; but only
in relation to others who have the power to confer upon the
individual an identity that constitutes personhood. This
position is the opposite of the concept of alienation, the
lonely ego, which underlies much Existentialist philosophy
and which has retained a strong hold on Western European
culture. His starting-point is theological rather than anthro-
pological: the doctrine of God rather than the doctrine of
man. It is, he argues, from the doctrine of the Trinity that we
are to derive our concept of personhood and our notion of the
relationship of the One and the Many.

> One of the striking peculiarities of St Basil's teaching on God,
> compared with that of St Athanasius and certainly that of the
> Western Fathers, is that he seems to be rather unhappy with
> the notion of substance as an ontological category and tends
> to replace it . . . with that of κοινωνία. Instead of speaking
> of the unity of God in terms of His one nature, he prefers to
> speak of it in terms of the *communion of persons*: communion
> is for Basil an ontological category. The *nature* of God is
> communion . . .[4]

Whether or not we accept his argument that the concept of
person enters our philosophical discourse (and our culture)
by way of the development of the doctrine of the Trinity in
Cappadocian theology, we cannot deny the powerful thrust
of the Cappadocians' teaching in the shaping of the specifically Christian understanding of the meaning of person, both
natural and supernatural; and the significance this might
have for the doctrine of the Church. If the essence of God is

communion, i.e. a unity arising out of a set of relationships, the Church must similarly be a communion and be understood, first, as a set of relationships: the body is defined by its interior relationships. Zizioulas makes the point: 'Now, when we look at the institutional aspect of ecclesiology, it follows that the institution that is supposed to express the unity of the Church must be an institution which expresses *communion*'. If this is correct, what implications might this have for the order and structuring of the Church?

One implication might be the abolition of all notions of hierarchy, and a recently published book of essays on the Church seems to propose this. Thus, for example, Colin Gunton, using the category of community provided by Zizioulas, takes issue with certain classical expositions of traditional Catholic church order, arguing that these derive either from models of civic organisations in which the necessity of authoritative government is of paramount concern or from a neo-platonic philosophical schema in which the Church's hierarchical structure mirrors the gradations of reality in the supernatural world.[5] Whereas, he argues, if the concept of *community* is primary and the model for the Church's life is the Trinity, there can be no given hierarchy already in place into which individual members are introduced. What seems to be favoured is a kind of free association in the Spirit in which structures are expressive of the kind of community which is created by the relationships of individual Christians who have heard the Word of God. No particular ordering of the relationships can be seen as a theological necessity. The essay might be read as a strongly argued case for a certain kind of Congregationalism into which the theological principles of Zizioulas have been introduced and cleverly applied. Gunton's argument is one of the clearest modern statements of a venerable basic Protestant criticism of Catholic ecclesiology: community precedes hierarchy.

However, it is not only Protestant scholars who have shown hostility to the idea of hierarchy. The long history of 'centralist' government in the Roman Catholic Church (and the unhappy experience of insensitive authoritarianism) has frequently issued in severe criticisms of the notion of hierarchy in Catholic writings. Christian Duquoc, for instance, in a book entitled *Provisional Churches*, interpreted the notion in an entirely negative way, seeing it as a legalistic concept and identifying it unequivocally with the exercise of a particular kind of oppressive power.

> After the blossoming of Catholic ecclesiology in the decades before the Second Vatican Council we have seen a theological and ecclesiological void. The theologians from before the Second Vatican Council drew attention to the lack of equilibrium in Catholic theology contrary to the intentions of the theologians of the early and medieval church; this was organized around the idea of hierarchy. This stress on the legalistic aspect, circumscribing the church's mediation of the priestly ministry, forgetful of the equality of believers by virtue of their participation in the universal priesthood of Christ through the gift of the Holy Spirit, arose out of the struggle against the Protestant Reformation.[6]

It is an interesting statement, typical of much Catholic unease with the way in which the hierarchy conducts itself towards the laity. It is typical too, in its confusion on the matter of order. To argue, as he seems to be doing, that the *hierarchical* ordering of the church came about as the result of the deliberations of the Council of Trent, and in an effort to combat the ecclesiological claims of the Reformers, is to interpret the notion in a naive and misleading way. Even the most casual reading of the theology of the 'early and medieval church' reveals that the hierarchical organisation was simply assumed; and where it was not assumed it was positively defended. How else can one make sense of Irenaeus' *Ordo Prebyterii* or Cyprian's *De Unitate*? One sees the concept of hierarchy entering ecclesiology as early as the letters of Ignatius of Antioch at the beginning of the second century. One may disapprove of it and think that a mistake has been made, but it is there, (perhaps even in Paul's metaphor of the Church as the Body of Christ) and it will not do to 'lay the blame' for hierarchical ordering at the feet of those who countered the ecclesiology of the Reformers at the Council of Trent. What did happen after the Council, of course, was

the increasing clericalisation of the church and the centrali-
sation of its authority in the Papacy. But that is to interpret
the idea of hierarchy in a particular way. And here, it must be
admitted, Duquoc could be correct, for the original meaning
of the word 'hierarchy' is 'rule by the priests': a concept that
would be foreign to the thought of Paul, Ignatius and
Irenaeus. The 'order' they envisaged was certainly not government by a priestly caste, though this came to pass in many
parts of the church in the West in the Middle Ages: and if
one were to interpret hierarchy in this sense only there could
be no argument for hierarchy in Christian community. But
one might argue, legitimately, for the developed and modern
usage of the word. Few people today recall that the original
meaning was 'priestly rule'. Nor does Duquoc mean exactly
that, for a little later in his book he contrasts a democratically
organised society with a hierarchically organised one to the
detriment of the latter, as though the former guaranteed
freedom and the latter was synonymous with tyranny. In
some sense we are all caught in the trap of language: the word
'hierarchy', like the word 'feudal' is, as I have already said,
almost always automatically used as a term of abuse, and the
word 'democracy' as a word of approval. This returns us to
the shift in sensibility to which I referred at the start of this
essay: from the cosmological interpretation of reality to the
historical interpretation. Can there be no recovery of the
term? Can it offer no truths about proper relationships in the
community of the Church?

Before I try to recover what has been lost and reveal the
theological richness of the term, I must again recognise the
fact that, in the history of both church and state, the kinds
of things which all critics of hierarchy detest and reject as
inimical to Christianity, legalism, repression, totalitarianism
etc., can be more easily instituted in a society which is
hierarchically organised. But, unlike some theologians, I am
not convinced that what might be called a hierarchical structure is, in itself, evil. Everything depends on the nature of
the hierarchy i.e. the actual shape of the order and the way
it functions. It can, of course, be perverted, and, when

structure is allowed to take precedence over persons, free-dom is lost; when the hierarchy tries to establish a hegemony over the 'republic', evil flows.

III

In 1943 the Anglican poet and theologian, Charles Williams, addressed the question of order in an 'essay' he wrote for the periodical *Time and Tide*, entitling it 'A Dialogue on Hierarchy'.[7] It is cast in the form of a Socratic dialogue, and the philo-sophical discussion is conducted in a suitably mocking ele-vated style. But the intention is serious. It opens with a reference to a recent, public debate about equality: 'Did you by chance read, Eugenio . . . a dispute on equality and degree, where the Hierarchy and the Republic might be said almost to contend? And to which side did you lean in the affray?' Eugenio at first evades answering directly, but later accepts his interlocutor's insistence on the necessity for 'degree'. However, soon after, he comments: 'We are not to suppose that the hierarchy of one moment is likely to be that of the next. The ranked degrees of intelligence are continually reordered.' And when asked to explain what exactly he means he gives, deliberately, slightly absurd examples: 'He who is a good master of his craft in music may do ill enough in the theatre, and the Prime Minister must be docile to an expert scullion. Degree is the inbreathing and outbreathing of joy, but with every breath the joy changes. If every living creature is unique, it must necessarily be so.' The point is clear, and, one might have supposed, incontestable: there is a 'hierar-chy' of talents, and only the evil (or stupid) person is jealous of the abilities of others. The example from music is a good one. Most of us have very little talent in performance, how-ever much we may love the art of music and are vivified by it. We are the passive, though loving recipients of the talents of others and must honour them in their art. We do not envy their ability of technique and interpretation; we are subordi-nate to them, and the notion of equality or inequality is irrelevant in this context. One is not less joyful or fulfilled as

a person because one is not the equal of someone else in a
particular sphere. There is order here: we are subordinate in
the sense that they, the musicians, are the agents of our
happiness and the source of our fulfilment. But where we do
not envy, they must not be arrogant; they must realise that
we will, in our turn and in our unique ways, be the origin of
happiness in others. 'We are not to suppose that the hierarchy
of one moment is to be that of the next.' A striking illustration of the situation Williams was trying to portray may be
found in a scene from the life of Thomas More when he was
Lord Chancellor of England. As Lord Chancellor he conducted the affairs of State in the Great Hall at Westminster.
In the same hall, on the other side, sat his father conducting
the business of the King's Bench. The office held by Thomas
was far superior to that held by his father, yet, each day, as he
proceeded to his place he knelt before his father to ask his
blessing, a counterpoint of reverence and subordination. All
life is to be seen as a constantly shifting pattern of hierarchies, and for this shifting pattern the metaphor of the
republic may be used. In Williams's 'Dialogue', Eugenio's
companion says: '. . . if each creature is unique, he owes
discreet obedience to all others and all others to him; if each
is in the base and at the apex, zenith and nadir at once, this
great exchange of duty can only be summed so. The classless
Republic is a republic of hierarchies, and each hierarchy is
the fleshing out of ranked equalities.' The reconciliation of
the interests (and rights) of the individual and the group can
only be achieved in this apparently paradoxical assertion of
the co-inherence of the principles of the republic and those
of the hierarchy.

I would now go so far as to assert that there must be a
similar reconciliation between the historical and the cosmological interpretations of reality; that unless there is seen to
be a co-inherence of these two methods the proper ordering
of the Church cannot be achieved. The Church must be both
republican and hierarchical: it must interpret itself both
historically and cosmologically. It is easier in our age to assert
the republican nature of the Christian community, as I have

demonstrated; it is much more difficult to show its proper hierarchy, especially when I assert that the proper order of the Church is one that preserves the paradoxical principle of subordination without inequality. Equality is the principle of the republic: the historical interpretation of reality; subordination is the principle of the hierarchy: the cosmological interpretation of reality. How can these be reconciled? I am convinced, like many others writing today, that the doctrine of the Trinity is not simply a dogmatic formulation for theologians to discuss, but an indispensable presupposition for a genuinely Christian ecclesiology. A recent report by the House of Bishops of the Church of England on the controversial issue of the ordination of women to the priesthood stated the case plainly in relation to the doctrine of ministry: 'This inner fellowship of the Church, grounded in the life of the Holy Trinity, has to be maintained and manifested in the life of the Church'.[8] Can the theology of the Trinity, so useful for Colin Gunton in establishing a republican notion of the church, also provide us with a true understanding of the notion of hierarchy?

That *communion* which is *being* of the persons of the Holy Trinity describes a life which is both republican and hierarchical. It was around the mystery of this paradox that many of the bitterest controversies of the early church revolved. The inability to hold the two concepts together resulted in heresy. Arianism was a failure to recognise the republican principle: the refusal to give equal glory to the persons of the Son and the Spirit. Modalism was the failure to recognise the hierarchical principle: the inability to see that, unless there were real and different relations within the life of the Godhead, that life could not be called a communion at all. Modalism has often been the direction in which the Trinitarian theology of the Western church has tended, and in contradistinction to much of that theology I should want to maintain the doctrine that within the Trinity the Father is to be understood as the source of the Godhead and the ground of its unity: that there is an 'order' within the life of God and that this order is to be 'imaged' in the life of the Christian

community. I do not believe that in saying this I am deliver-
ing ecclesiology into the hands of the neo-platonists who try
to mirror an order of the celestial hierarchies in ecclesiastical
institutions. We do not even need the mystical theology of
the Pseudo-Dionysius to perceive the necessity for the hierarchical ordering of the Church; we need only to recognise
the nature of the personal being of God. That being, as the
Cappadocian fathers so clearly saw, was one in which the
Father is the cause (the *archē*) of the Son (in generation) and
of the Spirit (in procession). '. . . the Father out of love —
that is, freely — begets the Son and brings forth the Spirit.
If God exists, He exists because the Father exists, that is, He
who out of love begets the Son and brings forth the Spirit.'[9]
And perhaps we should not hesitate to speak of subordination here, for the Son is eternally obedient to the Father —
a free and loving submission; and the Spirit moves only to
accomplish the Father's will at the behest of the Son. But
while such subordination is evident, the equality of each
person is unimpaired: none can exist without the others. But
the unity flows from the source, the Father: it is not achieved
by a kind of democratic vote by the members of the divine
society each of whom has the same rights. The absurdity of
the use of the language of democracy and rights in this
context helps to make the point.

What the modern mind finds difficult to comprehend is
any situation in which obedience is not the result of compul-
sion and a curtailing of the freedom of the individual, nor any
situation in which subordination is not, at the same time,
humiliation. But such incomprehension would have puzzled
not only the Cappadocian fathers but also the writers of the
New Testament. St Paul's elaborate imagery of the Church
as the Body of Christ is an attempt to hold together the
notions of republic and hierarchy: the community of the
faithful is neither a democracy nor an autocracy, and the
developed theology of the Epistle to the Ephesians views
Christ as the Head of a body so differentiated as to guarantee
the full development of each member; but the body grows
downward from the Head. Only in order is the personality

free to develop. Hence the necessity of 'institution', however often sinful men and women use the institution as a means of oppression. It is interesting to note that the author of the first letter of St Peter does not think it self-contradictory to say, on the one hand, that the Church is 'a chosen race, a royal priesthood, a holy nation, God's own people . . .' (1 Pet. 2: 9) and to urge, on the other hand, that the younger 'be subject to the elder'(5: 5). At the same time, all must be clothed with 'humility toward one another': the republic and the hierarchy; subordination without inequality. I am simply trying to establish the principle that suspicion of the concept of order, on the basis that it threatens freedom, is a peculiarly modern phenomenon with no foundation in Christian theology, and is plainly contradicted by the doctrine of the Trinity.

In an unpublished essay written towards the end of his life Eric Mascall succinctly summarised much of what I have been trying to say :

> It is only too understandable that with the entry of the Church into the political order the image of the Church as the eucharistic community assembled around the table of the Lord, with each 'order' — bishop, presbyters, deacons and layfolk — performing its part in the one united action, should have given way to an image of the Church as an organisation, with officials arranged in carefully defined grades of importance . . . That the Church has a structure, with a pattern of relations between its members, is only to be expected from its nature as a society of human beings, and that this includes relations of 'sub-ordination' in the strict sense of the word is natural too; but that this involves degrees of 'importance ' in no wise follows. Indeed the very notion of 'importance' needs very careful examination in a religion whose Founder declared that he was as one who served and who washed his disciples' feet. And we have the Trinity itself to remind us that total dependence, in the begetting of the Son by the eternal Father, is compatible with complete equality of the Begotten with the Begetter .[10]

As Mascall points out, the concept of 'importance' is one which would need to be thoroughly exorcised before it could be used in the context of ecclesial order, yet it is frequently some such notion which haunts our conversation when we

address the question of order, so secularised and unsacra-
mental has our thinking become. The bishop seems to signify
nothing but leadership, and the orders of the Church nothing
other than a convenient arrangement for pastoral care. But
the bishop, for example, has no 'importance' other than
fulfilling the sacramental role of being the instrument of the
unity of the Church. His ministry rests upon his order; it does
not arise out of a personal talent or ability. He belongs to an
order which is there *both* to be a sign of, *and* to fulfil the
function of, the spiritual unity of the eucharistic people.
Furthermore, the proper order of the Church is not there for
purely pastoral convenience or practical administration (as
might be maintained by many Protestant and some Catholic
Christians). Here we return to the sacramental interpretation of reality: the necessity for the concrete signs of unity
in diversity. The co-inherence of the republic and the hierarchy, the historical and cosmological interpretations of reality, are figured forth in the Eucharist. In this act of worship
the Church is presented as the sacrament of the Kingdom.
The unity of the body is signified and made real by the
celebrant (the hierarchy), but he can have nothing to celebrate and no unity to give if there is no people to respond to
and affirm his presidency (the republic). That ministry and
order are interdependent is one of the theological insights
bequeathed to us by Ignatius of Antioch: there can be no
bishop without the Church and no church without the
bishop. It is a matter of theological perception: and what is
being perceived is the doctrine of the Trinity. Only when that
theology is recovered will we again be able to see and experience what the early Christians saw and experienced: that
'the outward forms and images of the visible Church were
sacramental of the inner life of the invisible and mystical
Church where Christ reigned in glory'.[11]

Notes

1. E. Burke, *Reflections on the French Revolution*, originally published 1790.
2. J. Moltmann, *The Church in the Power of the Spirit*, (English translation SCM, 1977), p. 38.
3. Rowan Williams, 'The Nature of a Sacrament', *Signs of Faith, Hope and Love* (St Mary's Bourne Street, 1987), p. 35.
4. John Zizioulas, 'Christ, the Spirit and the Church', *Being as Communion* (Darton, Longman and Todd, 1985), p. 134.
5. 'The Church on Earth: The Roots of Community', *On Being the Church*, edited by Colin E. Gunton and Daniel Hardy (T. & T. Clark, 1989).
6. C. Duquoc, *Provisional Churches*, p. 18.
7. Charles Williams, *The Image of the City*, essays edited by Anne Ridler. (OUP, 1958).
8. General Synod Publications. GS764. 1987, p. 7.
9. John Zizioulas, 'Personhood and Being', op. cit., p. 41.
10. Eric Mascall, 'Ministry and Priesthood: A Catholic Statement' (unpublished).
11. Gareth Bennett, 'The Bishop as a Focus of Unity', *To the Church of England* (Churchman Publishing, 1988), p. 157.

2

Foundations for an Ecclesiology of Ministry

Robert Hannaford

In addressing the question of a theology of ministry, the theologian faces a range of problems, some theological and others conceptual. Since theology involves the application of critical reason to the Christian experience of salvation and its expression in the life of the Church, one cannot avoid confronting the demand for clarity and coherence. Hence I shall begin this essay by identifying and isolating the grammar of the language of ministry. Once we have a clear picture of the extent and limits of the idea of ministry, we can then begin the task of situating it within the being and life of the Church. As will be clear from the choice of title, the direction of the essay is founded upon the conviction that ministry can only be understood adequately if it is set within the context of an understanding of the Church itself.

In a short essay such as this it would be impossible to offer anything like a comprehensive theology of ministry. Instead we shall address a limited range of questions with a view to establishing the parameters for what might be termed a fundamental theology of ministry. Obviously there are important pastoral and theological issues about the nature and practice of ministry that need to be confronted. However, in order for these to be resolved, work needs to be done on the grounds for a theology of ministry. It is this that will concern us.

The Shape of the Problem

The rediscovery of a broader and more inclusive conception of ministry has become a matter of crucial concern for the contemporary church. Various factors play a part, ecumenism, new patterns in mission and evangelism, and the increasing difficulty in meeting the financial cost of a stipendiary clergy. Although there have been repeated calls for fresh thinking on this matter, most recent work on ministry, especially as it arises out of the ecumenical movement, has concentrated almost exclusively on the ministry of the ordained. There is, however, another, perhaps less vocal, imperative at work, and it is identified with the desire to recover what J.M. Barnett has described as the organic understanding of the Church. Barnett argues that over the centuries the Christian Church has lost the New Testament and Patristic model of the Church as a relational body, united sacramentally in a common fellowship and mission.[1] The earlier model of ministerial differentiation within a body conceived as an organic unity was gradually replaced by one in which differentiation was absolutised and taken as determinative for the Church's identity. The relation between clergy and laity was gradually polarised, with the former becoming a distinct and separate ministerial caste, seen as drawing its authority from Christ independently of the rest of the Church.

In an effort to overcome the concentration of ministry in the hands of the clergy attempts are now being made to widen the scope of the term itself. While this is to be welcomed there are signs that this new wine is often being poured into old sacks. Slogans such as 'every-member ministry' are not without their problems. Although there is a growing recognition that ministry rests upon the sacrament of baptism, and not exclusively upon that of orders, the suspicion remains that this slogan reflects the very individualism it is intended to replace. One of the difficulties of the clericalised view of ministry is that it is seen primarily as a gift of office bestowed upon individuals and therefore as something distinct from the life of the majority of Christian believers. In attempting to overcome this we must not perpetuate the problem simply by enlarging an un-revised individualistic understanding of ministry so as to include the whole Church. If 'every-member ministry' simply means that every Christian has his or her own ministry, the result is a radically individualistic understanding of the Church itself and not a genuinely expanded theology of ministry. It will be the argument of this essay that while ministry is a gift bestowed upon individuals it nonetheless arises out of the character and identity of the whole Church.

The apparent ease with which the term 'ministry' falls from the lips of Christian believers is deceptive. It suggests that the term's meaning is clear and non-controversial. However, several recent publications have pointed to the confusion that exists in the contemporary discussion of ministry.[2] A simple consideration of the breadth of ideas covered by the term suggests as much. It is used as a synonym for the ordained and also as a catch-all term for something that is said to be the common responsibility of all Christians. Then again, ministry is said to include certain clearly defined rôles within the Church such as leadership, preaching, teaching, and the administration of the sacraments, but it is also said to include certain 'normal' Christian activities like prayer and basic care within the community. The problem appears to be that the same term does service both for what is common to all Christians *and* for what differentiates within the Christian community. In the words of Helen Oppenheimer, ministry is a 'greedy concept'.[3] It is used so inclusively that it 'becomes impossible to sort out what is not ministry'.[4] The danger with a concept that appears to cover everything is that it lacks definition and coherence. As Oppenheimer puts it: 'Unless ministry can be distinguished from something else which is not ministry, it seems hardly worth talking about.'[5]

In an important new study, John N. Collins identifies the modern church's appropriation of the ancient Greek idea of *diakonia* as the basis of this confusion.[6] Collins argues that a whole generation of scholars, beginning with H.W. Beyer in his influential essay on *diakonia* in Kittel's *Theological Dictionary of the New Testament*, has taken the term to mean something equivalent to lowly or humble service.[7] Since *diakonia* is taken as the governing term for ministry this has had a major influence on the modern church's understanding of itself. Not only has the term 'ministry' itself been equated with humble service, and hence had its meaning broadened to include virtually every Christian task or responsibility, it has also influenced ecclesiology in a much broader sense, leading a whole generation of writers to view ministry or *diakonia* as the service that a servant church owes to the world. Very few New Testament scholars have questioned this approach to *diakonia*. Dieter Georgi's study of the opposition to Paul in 2 Corinthians is a notable exception to this. Georgi insists that *diakonia* is not a distinctively Christian term, and that its primary meaning has nothing to do with the duty of service to one's neighbour. After examining classical parallels he argues that *diakonia* should be understood as referring to the service performed by those whom God has chosen to be vehicles for transmitting his revelation.[8] Collins's study is, however, the first sustained attempt to challenge the tradition of interpretation established by Beyer.

In his book Collins examines the New Testament texts in the light of references to *diakonia* and its cognates in classical literature. He rejects the association of the term, by scholars, such as Edward Schweizer and C.F.D. Moule,[9] with humble service at table, arguing instead that in non-Christian sources the term is most often used to denote the carrying of messages or action as an emissary. It is this, Collins argues, that lies behind the meaning of the term in the New Testament. Words such as *diakonos*, *diakonia*, and *diakonein* 'do not speak directly of "attitude" like "lowliness" but express concepts about undertakings for another, be that God or man, master or friend'.[10] This conclusion leads Collins to offer a new reading of *diakonia* which slants it in a theological rather than an ethical direction:

> In Christian writings ... the verb (*diakonesai*) always signifies
> carrying out a task established either by God, by the terms
> of an ecclesiastical office, or by the authority of an apostle or
> by an authority within the community, in all cases with the
> special connotation of the sacred that characterises so much
> of its use in all senses and that of its cognates in non-Christian
> sources, and which leads Paul to designate both his own
> apostolic task and the spiritual functions of all Christians as
> 'ministries' or *diakonia*.[11]

Although some might take exception to the theological sub-
text in Collins's study[12] his exegetical work on *diakonia* in the
New Testament, and particularly his view that it should be
understood as a duty imposed by divine authority, has an
important bearing upon our concerns. First, his deconstruc-
tion of the ethical slant given to *diakonia* in the modern
discussion of ministry gives substance to the claim of Avery
Dulles and others that this has not only radically undermined
the Church's sense of its divine mission but also misrepre-
sented the biblical testimony on ministry.[13] Secondly, his
location of *diakonia* or ministry within the grammar of language to do with action on behalf of an authority helps to give
sharper focus to a term that has become dangerously vague.[14]
Finally, and most significantly, Collins's exegetical work further undermines the confident individualism of much modern thinking on ministry.

The last point is particularly important. Modern discussion has tended to locate ministry within the ethical domain
of general service or benevolence. The problem with this is
that ministry is detached from its theological basis in the
divine commission bestowed upon the whole Church and is
attached instead to the ethical responsibilities shared by all
Christians. The axis of thinking on ministry has shifted from
the collective life of the community to the life and duty of
Christian individuals. A feature of the ecclesial life of the
Christian community is confused with the obligations shared
in common by all believers: ministry becomes a general
ethical responsibility binding upon individuals and not a
specific action undertaken on behalf of God and his Church.
When *diakonia* is interpreted as humble service and treated

as an ordinary, and indeed univocal, feature of Christian life, it becomes impossible to distinguish not only between ordained and non-ordained ministry but also between what is and is not ministry. Ministry becomes part of the undifferentiated responsibility of all Christian individuals.

Collins's recognition that ministry is an ecclesially sanctioned and authorised act is a first step towards conceptual clarification. As we have seen, when too much is included in the concept, 'ministry' in the words of Thomas Franklin O'Meara 'fades away'.[15] The seriousness of the task that confronts the Church in working out an effective theology of ministry cannot be doubted. The contemporary experience of ecumenical dialogue on this matter illustrates the scale of the problem but it also offers an opportunity to identify a way forward. Most recent ecumenical work on ministry has focused on the narrower question of holy order or ordained ministry. The reason for this is fairly clear: the doctrine of ordained ministry and the mutual recognition of such ministries is one of the remaining areas of major disagreement between the churches. However, the disproportionate attention given to ordained ministry has served further to entrench the clericalised view of ministry. The theology of ministry is usually discussed in two parts, first, the theology of the ordained, and then, as an afterthought, the theology of the laity. Thus little or no attention is given either to the foundation of ministry in the life of the Church itself, or to the sense in which ministry is a dimension of the life of the whole people of God. The problem is that the doctrine of ministry has customarily proceeded from hierarchology rather than ecclesiology.[16] The net effect is a narrowly one-sided and distorted view of ministry which is divorced from the collective life of the whole Church. In overcoming this we need to show that a theology of ministry, understood as action for and on behalf of the Church, is consistent with an understanding of the Church as an organic community, where ministerial differentiation contributes to and does not diminish the unity and coherence of the whole body.

The Foundational Ministry of Jesus

The foundation of all Christian ministry lies in the ministry of Jesus himself (Acts 4: 10–12). Mark heads his Gospel with a clear declaration of the focus and purpose of Jesus' ministry: 'Jesus came into Galilee preaching the gospel of God, and saying "The time is fulfilled, and the kingdom of God is at hand; repent and believe in the gospel." ' (Mark 1: 14 f)[17] Although many New Testament scholars doubt that these are actually Jesus' words, there is general agreement that the synoptic gospels see the proclamation of God's Kingdom as the basis of Jesus' teaching and ministry.[18] In sayings, parables, miracles, and above all in his passion and death, Jesus is portrayed as the one who brings to fulfilment God's promise of peace and salvation.

Although the salvation-historical approach to biblical interpretation is currently unfashionable, it remains the case that the Christian Church has always regarded the earthly ministry of Jesus as the culmination of God's plan reflected in the story of the people of Israel. Jesus' proclamation of the Kingdom is understood as the fulfilment of the prophetic hopes of Israel.[19] It is this belief in an unfolding plan that led the Church to 'appropriate' the Hebrew Scriptures as its Old Testament, and the Christian reading of the Israelite experience of God is already evident in the New Testament itself. While the phrase 'the Kingdom of God' is not found in the Old Testament, there are many references to the kingship or rule of God,[20] and New Testament scholars have pointed to the existence of widespread messianic expectation in first-century rabbinic Judaism. The roots of belief in the divine Kingdom lie in the ancient Near-Eastern myth of the God who demonstrates kingly power by creating the world out of primeval chaos.[21] Israel modified and adapted this myth by incorporating it into its own experience of exodus and covenant. In the Old Testament we find a fusion of the idea of the divine kingship over nature and kingship demonstrated through history. It is against this background that the synoptic writers portray Jesus as the one who heralds the dawning of the age to come and the establishment of God's reign.

What did Jesus mean by the Kingdom of God? Although it is a recurrent theme throughout his teaching Jesus nowhere explains its precise meaning. Indeed, he is sometimes portrayed as declaring that it is a 'secret' only revealed to a few (for example, Mark 4: 11–12; Matthew 13: 11; Luke 8: 10). In historical terms it is obviously very difficult for us to be clear what exactly Jesus' hearers would have understood by the term. Clearly in speaking of the Kingdom Jesus was using a term that would have been familiar to his audience. However, Jesus' preference for parabolic forms of teaching suggests a deliberate reserve on his part. We know that the 'Kingdom of God' does not refer to a place or a human institution. The Hebrew term *malkuth* which lies behind the New Testament expression refers to the reign of God. The Kingdom of God is not anywhere or anyplace; it is a reference to or symbol of the sovereignty and power of God manifested in human history. Although the gospels make it clear that the Kingdom is in some sense present in the ministry of Jesus, they also suggest that it is distinct from all human societies. In other words, the Kingdom of God is understood as an eschatological reality. Although it is making its presence felt in the ministry of Jesus, it remains an experience of that which is inescapably ultimate and final. Jesus heralds its coming but, although in one breath it can be described as 'at hand' or 'present' (Mark 1: 9, 15; 13: 30; Matthew 10: 23), it is also that which can be said to await its final consummation (Mark 13: 32; Matthew 6: 10). The interpretation of the eschatological character of the Kingdom is a subject of ongoing debate amongst scholars.[22] What are often overlooked in this debate are the theological implications of the Kingdom's identification with the sovereignty of God. If the Kingdom is God's presence in the world as the hope of all creation, then it will always remain an experience of that which is ultimate and therefore mysterious (Mark 4: 11–12). Even in its consummation the Kingdom will remain an experience of that which is eschatologically distinct.

Karl Barth reacted against ethical interpretations of the Kingdom, insisting that Christianity is consistently and completely eschatological in character.[23] However, he can be accused of neutralising New Testament eschatology by eliminating any discussion of its temporal and historical character. Barth saw eschatology as an expression of the dialectic between time and eternity. The weakness of this is that the biblical conception of divine transcendence is transformed into a philosophical category. Walter Kasper is surely nearer to the truth when he describes the eschatological dimension of the Kingdom as an expression of the mystery of 'God's eternal decree of salvation, unfathomable for man, which will be made manifest at the end of the world'.[24] Eschatology, and not a philosophical conception of transcendence, is the New Testament's device for enshrining the ultimate mystery of the Kingdom. From a theological point of view it is, therefore, ultimately vacuous to ask whether or not the Kingdom is present or to come. The simple answer is that it is always a demonstration of the mysterious presence of the ultimate. As Kasper powerfully expresses it:

> Now is the time for the coming of God's kingdom; that is, the present is modified by the fact that the coming of the kingdom has begun and faces men with a choice. The kingdom, in other words, is the power which controls the future. It is now forcing a choice, and in this way is active in the present and totally determines it.[25]

Although so far we have only spoken of the ministry of Jesus as it is portrayed in the synoptic gospels, there is an important sense in which the reality to which Jesus' symbol of the Kingdom points remains a common focus throughout the pages of the New Testament. In order to grasp this we need to look in more detail at the question of the relationship between Jesus and the Kingdom. Ernst Troeltsch once wrote: 'Jesus did not bring the kingdom of God; the kingdom brought Jesus.'[26] This is altogether too simple a reading of the New Testament evidence. It is clear that the synoptic gospels sometimes portray Jesus as a preacher or messenger, pointing to something greater than himself. At other times, however, they hint at a much stronger link between Jesus and the Kingdom. Much here depends upon a resolution of the

debate, already alluded to, about the interpretation of New
Testament eschatology. In a significant survey of recent work
George Eldon Ladd insists that there is a growing consensus
that the kingdom of God must be understood as both present
and future in the teaching of Jesus.[27] Jesus is not only the
herald of a hope yet to be fulfilled: he is, at the same time,
the realisation of that hope. We can properly speak of the
existence of a dialectical relationship between Jesus and the
Kingdom. In his book *Jesus of Nazareth* Gunther Bornkamm
points out that the Greek term *basileia* [kingdom] can be used
synonymously with God himself.[28] The proclamation of the
Kingdom is the declaration of the presence of God himself.
In Jesus' person and ministry the Kingdom of God has
become an event in human history.[29] The reality which the
writers of the synoptic gospels refer to under the heading of
the 'Kingdom' is described elsewhere in the New Testament
as 'salvation', 'grace', and 'redemption', all of which are words
that speak of the presence of God as gift and healing. It is
not illegitimate to see Ephesians 1: 9, for example, as a gloss
on the reality of the Kingdom:

> For he has made known to us in all wisdom and insight the
> mystery of his will, according to his purpose which he set
> forth in Christ as a plan for the fullness of time, to unite all
> things in him, things in heaven and things on earth.
>   In him, according to the purpose of him who accomplishes
> all things according to the counsel of his will, we who first
> hoped in Christ have been destined and appointed to live for
> the praise of his glory.[30]

New Testament passages about the mediatorial rôle of Christ
in creation represent a re-focusing and a universalisation of
Jesus' ministry as redeemer. 'They are', in the words of
Walter Kasper, 'meant to bring out the eschatological-defini-
tive and universal character of the person and work of Jesus
Christ as the fullness of time . . .'[31] Jesus is the culmination
of God's plan for final salvation. In fellowship with Christ the
whole creation is already being drawn into the unity and
peace which has been God's plan since the foundation of the
world. John's Gospel addresses the same reality but de-

scribes it as eternal life: 'For God so loved the world that he gave his only Son, that whoever believes in him should not perish but have eternal life' (John 3: 16). Moreover Jesus is not only the agent of eternal life: union with him *is* eternal life: 'And this is eternal life, that they know thee the only true God and Jesus Christ whom thou hast sent' (John 17: 3). Jesus is not only the herald of God's Kingdom, he is also, in Origen's powerful phrase, *autobasileia*, the Kingdom in person.[32]

Jesus is minister of the Kingdom as herald and prophet but he is also minister in a much more direct sense. The Kingdom is no longer simply a promise for the future. In Christ it is already being incorporated into history. As L.S. Thornton puts it: 'It is not simply proclaimed in expectation and promise. It is present in fulfilment; for it is a present reality to the mind of Jesus.'[33] Jesus does not just proclaim a reality that lies in the future; he is the one through whom God is bringing about the realisation of the eschatological promise of salvation for all things. He not only taught 'as one who had authority' (Matthew 7: 29); he is also the one whom even the winds and sea obey (Matthew 8: 27). Jesus is not simply a messenger of salvation; he it is who has power and authority to forgive sins and to raise the sick from their beds (Matthew 9: 6). Christ is first to be born from the dead but he is also the ground and source of resurrection for all (1 Corinthians 15: 20–24). Jesus is agent or minister of God's kingdom as its means of fulfilment as well as its herald. He is the substance of the message that he came to proclaim for, as Walter Kasper puts it, 'Person and cause cannot be separated in Jesus. He is cause in person.'[34]

The Church's Ministry and the Kingdom

Although Jesus' preaching of the Kingdom provides what Thomas Franklin O'Meara has described as the 'primal force behind ministry', it would be fatal to overlook the uniqueness of Jesus' own relation to the Kingdom. In the past serious difficulties have been caused by basing the discussion

of the Church and its ministry on an absolute identification
of Church and Kingdom.[35] There is an important sense in
which Jesus is the Kingdom in person but this cannot be said
of the Church, at least not without certain crucial qualifications.

Establishing the nature of the link between the Church's
ministry and that of Christ depends upon a resolution of the
difficult question of the relationship between the Church
and the Kingdom. It is evident that the earliest generations
of Christians regarded the Kingdom as eschatological, and,
therefore distinct from any human institution, the Church
included. In this respect the ancient prayer from the *Didachē*
is typical: 'Remember, Lord, Thy church, to . . . gather it
together in its holiness from the four winds to thy Kingdom
which Thou hast prepared for it'.[36] Under Augustine's influence Catholic theology gradually came to identify the Kingdom with the Church.[37] Modern biblical scholarship has
called into question the historical accuracy of this interpretation of New Testament teaching. There are also serious
theological objections to be raised against treating Church
and Kingdom as synonymous. As an eschatological reality the
Kingdom can never be completely identified with any earthly
institution. The Kingdom is the coming into time of God's
promise for the last days and, as such, will always remain a
mystery, a reality of the age to come. The Kingdom is not at
the disposal of human beings. It is God's intervention in
history, his invitation to be conformed to the eschatological
promise of salvation and fulfilment.

Although the Kingdom is eschatologically distinct this
does not necessarily imply that there is no connection between the Church and the Kingdom. Yves Congar points out
that the Hebrew expression *malkuth* that lies behind the
Greek term *basileia* [kingdom] can be translated in two ways:
in an active sense as 'God's reign'; in a passive sense as 'the
Kingdom'.[38] While the Kingdom must be understood primarily in its active sense as the reign of God, we must not
overlook the need also to speak of it, especially at the *eschaton*,
as the *effect* of God's act.[39] The Kingdom is invitation and

promise but it is also fulfilment. It is not simply the subject of Christ's prophetic preaching: it is also the new state of reality brought about by the exercise of his kingly and priestly power. In other words, Congar invites us to contemplate the Kingdom not only as invitation and promise but also as 'an order of things in which man and creation will be condemned to the will of God'.[40] In this order 'All things will be gathered under Christ as their one head; a single, hierarchical, total order, consequent on the perfect dominance of the higher principle over the lower elements, and finally on perfect dominance of the *Pneuma*, the gift that belongs to the messianic era.'[41] In the resurrection of Jesus and in the gift of the Holy Spirit the promise of the Kingdom is already having its effect:

> He is the head of the body, the church; he is the beginning, the first born from the dead, that in everything he might be pre-eminent. For in him all the fullness of God was pleased to dwell, and through him to reconcile all things, whether on earth or in heaven, making peace by the blood of his cross (Col 1: 18–20).

Congar's identification of the Kingdom in terms of what might be described as the twin modes of promise and fulfilment provides us with an appropriate vehicle for reassessing the relationship between the Kingdom and the Church.

Although the Church is not synonymous with the Kingdom, it is the community of those who are already experiencing the promised reconciliation of all things. It is the first tangible effect of Jesus' preaching of the Kingdom. However, the Church does not only exist in the mode of the Kingdom's fulfilment: it is also called to a prophetic ministry of proclamation. The Church exists because before the end comes 'the gospel must first be preached to all nations' (Mark 13: 10).[42] The Church's preaching of the gospel is, as Cranfield describes it, an eschatological event.[43] God uses the Church, in its proclamation of the gospel, as a sign and witness of his Kingdom. There is a tendency on the part of some theologians, Congar included, to see the two modes of the Kingdom as two stages, separated in time. While the observation that the Church exists in the 'between-times' has assisted theologians in recapturing the eschatological positioning of the Church, it would be wrong to see promise and fulfilment simply as two temporal stages in the successive development of the history of the Church. It is more fruitful to think of promise and fulfilment as two modes of the Kingdom in dialectical relation with one another. They are dialectical in the sense that they are distinct but mutually constitutive ways in which the Kingdom manifests itself. The Kingdom as promise is precisely the promise of fulfilment. From this point of view the Church cannot be said to inhabit an interim stage in the history of salvation; the Church is, rather, a community of both promise and fulfilment.[44] Even in its ministry of proclamation, when the Church acts as a declaratory instrument of the promise of fulfilment in the age to come, it already experiences in its own life the substance of that promise. The earnest of that promise is the Pentecostal gift of him who both recalls to mind all that Christ did (John 14: 26) and makes known the things that are coming (John 16: 13). Along the same lines the author of Mark's Gospel states that when Christians fulfil their ministry it is not they who speak but the Holy Spirit (Mark 13: 11), the same Spirit whose advent is the principal sign of God's Kingdom come in power. Furthermore, the community of Christians is promised that the suffering this ministry of proclamation will bring them is part of the birth pangs of the Kingdom (Mark 13: 12–13). In ministry the Church is both an instrument of the Kingdom and a sign of its realisation. The Church is not simply a bare vehicle for the proclamation of the Kingdom: in its ministry it also anticipates the very promise that it proclaims.

We might then speak of the Church as having what G.E. Ladd describes as a 'dual character'.[45] In this age the Church is subject to persecution and the limitations imposed by human sinfulness, but even in its tribulation it already anticipates the power of the age to come. Although in its body the Church experiences the Lord's *pasch*, it is already the recipient of the Spirit, the final gift of the risen and ascended

Lord. It is the Church's character as an anticipation of the fulfilment of the Kingdom that lends urgency to Christ's teaching about the need for lowliness and humility on the part of his disciples. Concern for greatness and position, while seemingly natural to this age, is a contradiction of the life of the Kingdom (Mark 10: 35 ff). Although the Church in this age can never expect fully to attain perfection, it is nonetheless called to bear witness to the perfect order of the Kingdom.[46]

Ministry and the Sacramental Identity of the Church

We have spoken of the Church's ministry as an expression of Jesus' ministry of the Kingdom. However, although the Church expresses the Kingdom as both promise and fulfilment, and in that sense reflects the ministry of Jesus, he alone is the Kingdom in person. Christ and the Church are heralds and instruments of the Kingdom but he is uniquely its source and principle. The New Testament affirms the unity between Christ and the Church but it is careful to do this in language that maintains the distinctiveness of Christ as head of the body (Ephesians 1: 22–23; 4: 15–16; 5: 23–27). Christ is both Lord *in* the Church and Lord *over* the Church.[47] The question now arises as to how this insight can be incorporated into a coherent ecclesiology: In what sense does the Church 'express' the Kingdom, and how can this be explained adequately without usurping the unique ministerial and mediatorial rôle of Jesus? It is to this question that we now turn.

We have already defined 'ministry' as action by the Church or its agents on behalf of the Kingdom. Talk of ministry as 'action' is potentially misleading. It could all too easily suggest a functionalist understanding of the nature of the Church and its task. A.T. and R.P.C. Hanson were right to question functional or utilitarian theories of the Church in their recent Anglican ecclesiology.[48] However, when insisting that one can only ask what the Church is and not what it is for, they were surely mistaken. A non-functionalist account of the Church is not inconsistent with the claim that the Church's identity is tied to its purpose or mission. Quite the contrary: we cannot hope to understand the being of the Church, which the Hansons regard as primary, without paying due regard to its purpose. Separating questions about the Church's identity from the discussion of its purpose only serves to give the impression that the Church's being somehow precedes its mission.

The high-priestly prayer of Jesus in John's Gospel contains a passage with enormous significance for our understanding of the ministerial character of the Church:

> I do not pray for these only, but also for those who believe in me through their word, that they may all be one; even as thou, Father, art in me, and I in thee, that they also may be in us, so that the world may believe that thou hast sent me. The glory which thou hast given me I have given to them, that they may be one even as we are one, I in them and thou in me, that they may become perfectly one, so that the world may know that thou hast sent me and hast loved them even as thou hast loved me (John 17: 20–23).

This passage cuts across the rather sterile debate about functional versus ontological definitions of the Church. It is the Church's being as a community at one with its Lord that is stressed throughout this prayer. At the same time, this communion is identified as having a clear purpose, 'that the world may believe'. The Church's being or nature cannot be established by prescinding from the question of its purpose. The Church is constituted as a communion or unity whose mission or ministry it is to participate in the reconciliation of all things in Christ.

Many theologians, especially those in the Catholic tradition, see the sacramental model of the Church as a way of conceiving the Church that avoids the ontological-functional divide.[49] A further strength, as we shall see, is that it provides the basis for a dynamic understanding of the union in distinction of the unique ministry of Christ and the Church's ministry.

Although the sacramental view of the Church was anticipated by early theologians such as Cyprian and Augustine, it is only in this century that it has emerged as a significant area of enquiry. Henri de Lubac played a crucial rôle in this recovery. De Lubac summarised this conception of the Church as follows:

> If Christ is the sacrament of God, the Church is for us the sacrament of Christ; she represents him, in the full and ancient meaning of the term, she really makes him present. She not only carries on his work, but she is his very continuation, in a sense far more real than that in which it can be said that any human institution is its founder's continuation.[50]

Karl Rahner further developed this idea, describing the Church as the 'primal' or 'fundamental' sacrament.[51] Talk of the Church as the 'fundamental sacrament' is misleading, a point that Rahner later acknowledged.[52] As Eberhard Jungel, from the Protestant side, insists, talk of the Church as a sacrament must 'start with the fact that in the New Testament, *sacramentum* is nothing other than the eschatological mystery of the saving divine decree in favour of sinners which was enacted in the history of Jesus Christ'.[53] Walter Kasper concurs, arguing that the terms 'primal' or 'fundamental' sacrament should be applied to Christ alone.[54] Although the Church is a sign or instrument of Christ's primal ministry, it should not be conceived in terms that appear to usurp his unique rôle and status. He alone is the foundation of the Kingdom, and it is, therefore, appropriate to think of the term 'sacrament' as primarily christological in scope and as ecclesiological in only a derivative sense.

The Fathers of the Second Vatican Council used the sacramental model, alongside others, in the Dogmatic Constitution on the Church *Lumen Gentium*. While acknowledging the distinction between the Church and the Kingdom the Constitution nonetheless describes the Church as 'the initial budding forth' of God's Kingdom.[55] Although the document does not use the sacramental model very frequently, its importance is underlined by being placed in a prominent position in the introductory section:

> By her relationship with Christ, the Church is a kind of sacrament or sign of intimate union with God, and of the unity of all mankind. She is also an instrument for the achievement of such union and unity.[56]

In a book pre-dating the Council Karl Rahner had already spoken of the intimate connection between the realisation of the mystery of salvation in Christ and the Church. He described the Church as the continuance of the salvific presence of Christ in the world.[57] The saving mystery of Christ only comes to fulfilment when it is realised in a community characterised by faithful response to the primal ministry of Christ, and it is this that led the Fathers of the Council to describe the Church as an 'instrument'. However, as a sacrament, the Church can appropriately be described as a fruit and effect of salvation as well as a cause and means of grace. The Church is both 'the sign which brings with it always and inseparably what it signifies' and a celebration of 'the eschatologically triumphant mercy of God'.[58] Its mission is to be the principal sign of God's kingly rule already active in the world.

A sacrament has what might be termed a dual aspect. Looked at from one point of view it manifests all the characteristics of created reality; from another it displays the qualities of a sign of un-created grace. In other words, it is characteristic of a sacrament to be both a token of the created order and a realisation of the new order of redemption and salvation in Christ. It seems to be a characteristic of a sacrament that the grace signified is always in a sense concealed or veiled. Sign and reality signified remain in an important sense distinct. It is because the Church also has this dual character that it is appropriately described as a 'kind of sacrament'. Constituted by Christ as a visible sign of salvation for all humankind, it is also a human society formed from the sinful flesh of Adam. This means, paradoxically, that while the Church points to the reality of salvation, it also illustrates the need for salvation. The Church lives under the sign of the cross even while it celebrates the resurrection of the Lord. Although it is the fruit of Easter and Pentecost the

Church awaits the final revelation of what it will be. It is this fact that determines ecclesial existence as a pilgrimage or discipleship of the cross. Salvation is both the Church's gift and its hope. While time allows the Church is always in mission, called to proclaim and to realise in its own life the gift of salvation which is both its ground and its goal.

The claim that sacraments have a dual character is reflected in the western distinction between the terms *res* and *sacramentum*. The *sacramentum* is the external or visible sign of the sacrament; the *res* is the internal reality of the sacrament, the grace that gives the visible sign its salvific power. The drawback to this traditional terminology is that it is ontologically rather than eschatologically conceived. It fixes sacramental language in the grammar of things rather than in that of event or promise and fulfilment. The assumption that the presence of God as the mystery of salvation can be adequately explained in terms of a distinction between external and internal reality fails to do justice to the incarnational principle that God is truly present in the visible humanity of Christ's body. Although that presence is a presence in mystery, it is not a presence that is simply internal. Classical christology decisively rejected the idea that the divine in Jesus was concealed in his body, like a ghost in a machine. God is revealed and not concealed by the flesh of Jesus Christ's body. It is true of course that in the incarnate Christ the God-Man is revealed only to those who have faith, but this does not mean that his divinity is somehow hidden beneath the historical and earthly form of Jesus' body. It is rather that in the incarnate one the second person of the Holy Trinity is present in the mode of anticipation. To those with faith the risen Lord is already acknowledged as the Lord of the Ages, and is experienced as such, but his final revelation awaits the *eschaton*. There is no ontological distinction between the historical Jesus and the Lord who is to come. The difference lies in the manner or mode of Christ's presence. Our suggestion is that the eschatological character of christology has direct implications for our understanding of the sacramental nature of the Church. The Church cannot be adequately understood if it is thought of as a bare external form that somehow both conceals and reveals an internal reality. God's Kingdom is both contained and revealed in the earthly, and thus visible, form of the human community of the Church.

What we have termed the dual-aspect theory serves to underline the crucial fact that our sacramental experience of Christ is after the manner of both remembrance and anticipation. Christians celebrate the presence of Christ in the eucharistic meal, but there is an important sense in which this is an anticipation of that moment when we shall see him face to face. The same point can be made by recognising that the Eucharist is both *anamnesis* and *epiclesis*.[59] It is both a celebration of the earthly life of Jesus and an anticipation of his coming in glory at the end of time. The Church, as a sacrament, is, as Rahner puts it, 'the official presence of the grace of Christ in the public history of the human race'.[60] At the same time, however, it is also an anticipation of that final redemptive community where God will be 'all in all'. In other words, it belongs to the Church's character as a sacrament to be both a sign of salvation now and an earnest of the fulfilment for which it too yearns.

The sacramental model of the Church serves to make explicit its identity and calling as the principal sign and instrument of the Kingdom. Ministry is not a function which the Church can choose either to embrace or not. It is a horizon of the whole Church, an expression of its identity as the sacrament of God's eschatological decision for human beings. Ministry should not then be understood as simply a consequence or implication of its calling and identity. Ministry is rather one of those characteristics that identifies the Christian community. It is a necessary and not a contingent condition of its existence. The Church's being or identity does not precede its calling to ministry on behalf of the Kingdom. On the contrary, ministry is, as Zizioulas puts it, 'constitutive of and not derivative from the Church's being'.[61] The Church's birth lies not just in Easter or Pentecost but also in the call of Christ to discipleship and ministry on behalf of the Kingdom. The Church becomes more truly what it already is when it obeys the Lord's command to 'make disciples of all nations, baptising them in the name of the Father and of the Son and of the Holy Spirit' (Matthew 28: 19). This is why ministry, even when we define it as *action* on behalf of the Kingdom, can never be defined simply in functional terms. Ministry belongs rather to the very being or identity of the Church.

The One-and-Many Ministry and Baptism

Lest we be accused of holding a merely abstract and an a-historical view of ministry we must turn in a moment to a discussion of the question of how ministry becomes visible as *action* in the life of the Christian community. Before we do so, however, we must clarify an important point that is already beginning to emerge. In identifying ministry as constitutive of the life and identity of the whole Church we are not suggesting that it does not also exist as a reality in the lives of individual members of the body of Christ. When, as a corrective to individualistic views of ministry, we insist that, before it is an expression of the specific calling of some, ministry is an aspect of the collective life of the whole Church, the expression 'before' should not be interpreted as suggesting either a temporal or a logical priority. In this context the term is used solely as a corrective. Ministry is neither wholly the prerogative of the one nor of the many. Rather we must speak of it as having a simultaneous reality both in the community itself and in its members. Maintaining a sense of this simultaneity is difficult, but a consideration of the significance of baptism for ministry may help to clarify the point.

The location of ministry within the very identity or being of the Church helps to explain the importance of baptism. It is popular at the moment to see baptism as constituting in itself a sort of general vocation to ministry. This is to be welcomed as a reminder of the calling to active responsibility in the Church bestowed by baptism. John Zizioulas, for example, argues that baptism and confirmation constitute an ordination, translating the newly-baptised into a specific *ordo* within the eucharistic community.[62] Zizioulas's view represents an advance on ecclesiologies, whether Catholic or Protestant, that treat the baptised lay state as providing no more than a 'generic source or principle' for the development of other states or orders within the Church.[63] Although theologies that ground holy order in baptism have the advantage of linking ordained ministry more firmly to the ministerial calling of the whole Church, the baptised state must not be seen as simply a background against which other forms of ministry develop. A view of baptism that reduces it to the category of an *a priori* condition or presupposition of ordained ministry cannot be right. While appearing to enhance the significance of baptism for the ministerial state it in fact undermines the dignity and importance of the lay baptised state. However, the view outlined by Zizioulas and others is not without its problems. If baptism is understood as admission into an order, what are we to make of the baptismal status of Christians who subsequently enter another order within the Church? If baptism is primarily admission into a specific *ordo* within the eucharistic community, does the baptismal calling of those admitted into the order of presbyters cease to have any significance? This would seem to be the case if, as Zizioulas insists, order depends entirely upon one's rôle and identity within the context of the Eucharist.

Treating baptism as primarily admission into an order within the Church, or, even more problematically, as bestowing an individual vocation, overlooks the primary significance of baptism as initiation into the community of the Church. Baptism represents neither admission into a fixed order nor the bestowal of a generic capacity for the reception of other orders. Baptism is important for ministry because it marks an individual's incorporation into the ministerial community of the Church. If baptism, which is given to all, is treated as something akin to ordination, we are once again in danger of loading too much onto the idea of ministry. As we have seen, when ministry is applied to the general Christian life of the baptised the danger is that the idea ceases to have any clear meaning. Baptism is important as a foundation for ministry because it is the sacrament that unites people with the Church. In other words, baptism incorporates a person into a community that has ministry as a constitutive part of its character or identity. Baptism does not, then, so much bestow a ministerial calling as call someone into the ministerial community of the Church.

In a major new study of lay ministry Kenan B. Osborne argues for discipleship as the ground and basis of all categories of Christian ministry, lay and ordained.[64] While this view has its attractions it too can be criticised for failing to observe the simultaneity that exists between the ministry of the one Church and the ministerial calling of specific individuals within that Church. Although both ministry and discipleship are a work for the Kingdom, it is important to draw a distinction between them. Discipleship is a common obligation of all the baptised, but ministry is by its nature a summons to some particular, explicit, work for and on behalf of the Church. Although the appeal to discipleship as the ground for ministry has the apparent advantage of opening up ministry to the laity, it is open to question whether this serves the intended purpose. In making Christian discipleship, which by its very nature is often a hidden or concealed work for the Kingdom, the foundation for lay ministry Osborne has once again made it difficult, if not impossible, to distinguish between what is and is not ministry. More fundamentally, in grounding ministry in what is a common feature of all Christian life, he has made it in some ways more difficult to clarify the involvement of the laity in action for and on behalf of the Christian community. Discipleship is what the individual owes as a duty towards God, whatever his or her specific order or calling, while ministry is an act performed at the instigation of the Church.

It is important, therefore, to observe a distinction between ministry and what we might describe as the observance of a normal Christian life. While we should welcome the insistence that ministry is not the exclusive preserve of the ordained, and that baptism marks the admission of a man or woman into a ministerial community, it does not follow that every action performed by a baptised person is a ministry. Christians who carry their discipleship into their place of work are undoubtedly performing a work on behalf of the Kingdom, but this is not necessarily a form of ministry. 'For', as Thomas Franklin O'Meara observes, 'life is not a direct public action, for life is not clear and explicit'.[65] Christian discipleship is a way of life, while 'ministry is something the Christian does explicitly for the Kingdom and the Church'.[66] We could add too that the explicit nature of ministry is an implication of the sacramental identity of the ministerial community of the Church. Ministry always exhibits the characteristics of a 'sign', while discipleship is often an implicit expression of the Christian gospel.

The Manifestation of Ministry

So far we have emphasised the sense in which ministry is a feature of the communal identity of the Church. We must now turn to a more explicit examination of the sense in which ministry finds its simultaneous expression in the lives of individual Christians. Ministry is part of the public life of the Church and not simply a constitutive feature of its character or being. In approaching this we need to re-examine what is involved in the claim that ministry is an aspect of the sacramental identity of the Church.

In an effort to give a clearer focus to the discussion of ministry we defined it tentatively as action on behalf of the Kingdom. The sacramental model of the Church and its ministry re-inverses this definition. Although a sacrament, as an anticipation of final salvation in God's Kingdom, reflects something of the mystery that shrouds the *eschaton*, it is also a visible *sign* of the same reality. As a sign and instrument of Christ's ministry of the Kingdom, the Church is a visible manifestation of that promise. The Church, that is, does not just have ministry as part of its identity or character; ministry is also made visible in the life and action of the community of believers. The same point can be said to emerge also from our earlier insistence upon the dual character of the Church as sacrament. Ministry belongs not only to the Church in its eschatological aspect as celebration of the Kingdom's fulfilment; it also belongs to its existence under the aspect of promise. Ministry, that is, comprises both the gift and the explicit task of the Christian community.

In any human community it is natural that some should exercise leadership or act on behalf of the rest of the community. Those who occupy such positions are normally selected for this rôle, and their inauguration is often marked by a form of public recognition or commissioning. The Church is no exception to this rule. Those who exercise a form of ministry are generally set apart for this task in some communal or public way, ordination being the clearest and most obvious instance of this. Speaking of the Kingdom as coming to visibility in the ministerial life of the human community of the Church has sometimes been regarded as problematic. In the past Protestant theology tended to draw a sharp distinction between the visible and the invisible church, regarding the latter as entirely interior, spiritual and transcendent. Eighteenth and nineteenth-century Catholic theology for its part witnessed a growing interest in the idea of the Church as the mystical body of Christ. As Henri de Lubac points out, this trend sometimes led to an exaggerated stress on the invisible nature of the God-ward dimension of the Church.[67] According to this view a distinction is drawn between the Church's external structure and what is believed to be its internal and animating form. The Church is understood as existing from an interior or mystical relation to Christ. All that has lasting and profound significance is attributed to the 'mystical body' concealed beneath the earthly body of the Church.

Superficially the distinction between a visible and an invisible church appears to offer a solution to the problem of how the Church can be both a sign of the promised Kingdom and a manifestation of its fulfilment. Or, to put the same point in different terms, it appears to offer a way of conceiving the Church as both a manifestation of God in his Kingdom and of human beings in their, albeit grace-filled, search for salvation. The difficulty is that the dualism set up between the invisible and visible, interior and exterior, soul and body, establishes a tension between the Church as a means and instrument of grace and as an ordered and structured human society. Under the one guise the Church is said to be a partaker in the divine nature; under the other it is said to be merely a sharer in fallen human nature. De Lubac points to the consonance of this dualistic way of thinking with early christological heresies. In ecclesiology, as in christology, we may distinguish two opposite errors, *monophysite* and *Nestorian* respectively. Against these, as de Lubac points out, 'We must remember that the human element itself, as something essential to the structure and life of the Church as Christ willed her to be, is divine in its foundation.'[68] It belongs to the very divine foundation of the Church that it is incarnated in the historical body of an earthly community. 'There then', writes de Lubac, 'is the Church — human and divine at once even in her visibility, "without division and without confusion", just like Christ himself, whose body she mystically is.'[69]

The Church that we actually experience as a community of human beings is not a cipher for an underlying reality supposedly concealed beneath the public surface of ecclesial life. It is precisely the living human community which is, as Paul so forcibly expressed it, 'His body . . . the Church' (Colossians 1: 24). One important advantage of the sacramental model of the Church lies in the fact that it balances the divine and human in the Church without resorting to dualism. Sacramental language allows us to affirm the revelatory potency of earthly and material things while acknowledging the eschatological distinctiveness of the realities signified. It is the visible earthly community of the Church that is the principal sign of Christ's continuing ministry of the Kingdom until he comes. Instead of a dualism of visible and invisible, which effectively denies significance to the life and order of the earthly Church, we have spoken of a sacramental dialectic between promise and fulfilment. The

Church as society and institution is both an instrument and sign of the promise of the Kingdom *and* an anticipation of its fulfilment. In this age the Church lacks the perfection of fulfilment, but she points to it and celebrates it already in the manner and mode of anticipation.

This way of thinking provides us with a theological framework for situating the practice of ministry in the life of the Church. The public or explicit nature of ministry is an expression both of the collective or organic nature of the Church and of its sacramentality. Indeed, the one principle tends to illuminate and re-inforce the other. The Church is sign or sacrament precisely as the body of Christ, the visible community that is formed into a unity by its sharing in the eucharistic celebration of the Kingdom: 'Because there is one bread, we who are many are one body for we all partake of the one bread'(1 Corinthians 10: 17). Describing the Church as organic involves, then, not only reference to its sociological structure as a complex human institution but also recognition of the specifically ecclesial or corporate nature of its identity as an instrument of the Kingdom. It is precisely in its public, communal, life that the Church is constituted as the sacrament of God's eschatological promise 'to reconcile to himself all things' (Colossians 1: 15–20).[70]

Lay and Clerical Ministry and the Dialectic of Promise and Fulfilment

It is not our intention in this essay to address the question of either a specifically lay or ordained category of ministry. Instead we are seeking the foundation for an ecclesiology of ministry. Nonetheless, in the context of our current discussion of the visible expression of ministry in the public life of the Christian community, we must confront an issue that has serious implications for the significance of lay ministry. We refer here to the tendency on the part of some theologians to equate the lay-clerical distinction with what we have termed the sacramental dialectic between promise and fulfilment.

A number of scholars who point to the dualism inherent in our sacramental experience have worked this out in terms of the Church's ministerial structures. De Lubac, for example, describes the Church under two aspects, one active, the other passive. Under the first the Church is 'the voice which calls her together, or the power that assembles, together with all the organs and all the "instruments" which are at its disposal for that purpose'.[71] Under the second it is 'the assembly once constituted'.[72] This reflects Augustine's distinction between the Church as the 'divine calling-together' and the 'community of the called-together'.[73] What de Lubac has in mind is the distinction between the Church as instrument of salvation and as community of those on the way to salvation. He describes the failure to observe this distinction as equivalent to a 'practical-purposes monophysitism'.[74] In other words, de Lubac understands the distinction as a reflection of the Church's 'two natures', the one human and the other divine.

De Lubac is careful to insist that the active-passive distinction applies to the visible and earthly society of the Church. However, his use of the language of 'two natures' in addressing the question has led him to ontologise a distinction that we have sought to present only under the aspect of eschatology. Adopting ontological language at this point makes it virtually inevitable that substantial terms will be used in identifying this distinction. One consequence of de Lubac's ontologising — albeit one which insists upon the union without confusion of the divine and human in the Church — is his fixing of this distinction in the structural differentiation of lay and ordained Christians. As de Lubac himself describes it:

> These distinctions concerned two categories of persons within the society of the Church, and without all covering the same ground they all convey one and the same duality which is essential to the structure of that society — pastors and flock, Church teaching and Church taught, Church ruling and governed, clergy and laity, hierarchy and faithful, ministers and subjects of sacraments — or, as was once said, *sacerdotes* and *idiotes*.[75]

Notwithstanding de Lubac's insistence upon the unity and integrity of the visible church, his articulation of the distinction between the Church as active and passive appears to incorporate into his ecclesiology the very monophysitism he was at pains to avoid. We now find that what de Lubac has termed the 'divinity' of the Church is associated with the clergy, and its 'humanity' with the laity. Here what we have described in terms of a dialectic is collapsed into a polarity of lay and ordained. In this presentation of the dual-aspect character of the Church there is a clear distinction of the 'two natures' of the Church but no real sense of their union in the whole body of believers. Failure to observe the sacramental dialectic of promise and fulfilment has led de Lubac to absolutise the separation between the two. The consequence of this for an understanding of the visible manifestation of ministry is fairly clear. The clergy alone are held to represent the Church as sacrament or minister of salvation, with the laity representing the Church as receiver of sacraments and community on the way to salvation. This overlooks the participation of the whole people of God in the celebration of the sacraments and in the ministry of proclamation. Furthermore, it understates the sense in which the clergy, no less that the laity, are children of the Church in which they are also honoured as fathers. At a more fundamental level it overlooks the fact that it is the whole community of the baptised, laity no less than clergy, that is constituted as the visible sacrament of salvation. It is the Church in its unity and diversity, as one and many, which is mysteriously both sign of the promised Kingdom and celebration of its fulfilment.

Identifying the sacramental dialectic in the ministerial life of the Church is a complex matter and it is all too easy to fall back on something approaching the rejected distinction between a visible and invisible church. However, in order to apply the principle of dialectic consistently, it is important to recognise that the entire life of the Church is a reflection of its sacramental identity as both promise and fulfilment. It is not possible to point, without ambiguity, to one element in the ministerial life of the Church as 'promise' and to another as 'fulfilment'.

Ministry and Charism

Any discussion of the manner in which ministry comes to visibility in the life of individuals within the Christian community would be incomplete without some discussion of the relationship between *charism* and ministry, and it is to this that we now turn. Attempts are sometimes made to contrast the supposed charismatic structure of the New Testament Church with the more formal ministerial structures of later Christianity. The inference is drawn that the latter somehow reflects a corruption of the primitive pattern of ministry.[76] The *charismata* are seen as expressions of a 'purer' libertarian Christianity, while an ordered ministry is portrayed as a legalistic corruption of this. In Protestant circles this has often been understood as an instance of the struggle within Christianity between gospel and law. One effect of this way of thinking has been the identification of ministry with individual Christian fulfilment rather than the collective and communal life of the Church. In Catholic theology, in contrast, it can be argued that such stress has been laid on ordered and hierarchical ministry that *charism* has been relegated to the margins of 'official' Church life. The net effect in both cases is the same: *charism* is divorced from ministry and treated as something spectacular and exceptional.

Recent scholarship, however, has suggested a more central, one might say ordinary or normal, rôle for the *charismata* in the life of the Christian community. Thomas Franklin O'Meara, for example, reminds us that Paul understood *charisms* as founded upon the fundamental experience of God in Christ: 'For the wages of sin is death, but the free gift (*charism*) of God is eternal life in Christ Jesus our Lord' (Romans 6: 23). *Charisms* are not exceptional for they are expressions of the ground from which all Christian life proceeds. As O'Meara puts it, 'None of these *charisms* is essentially miraculous or ecstatic but all are necessary aspects of

Church life.'[77] All are given for the 'common good' (1 Corinthians 12: 7) and for the building up of the body of Christ. In similar vein the New Testament scholar E. Käsemann insists that *charisms*, although diverse, are a universal phenomenon, and that they are always given to serve the needs of the Christian community:

> Our definition of *charism* is the concrete form and individuation of the grace of the Spirit, because every Christian is a partaker of grace and of the Spirit; it is implicit also in our account of the body of Christ which we described as being composed purely of *charismata* and of those endowed with them.[78]

Instead of seeing *charisms* as sparks of supernatural power or energy erupting against the strain of communal life we should see them as a gift of the Spirit that has ministry as its goal. 'Spirit', as O'Meara puts it, 'leads to ministry'.[79] *Charisms* are expressions of the Spirit-filled life of the ministerial community of the Church.

This is completely consistent with the picture of ministry as we have so far described it. Ministry is the proper and normal expression of *charism* in the life of the Church. Indeed speaking of ministry in terms of *charism* helps to correct an impression we might have given that ministry is simply a creation of the Church. Ministry is an action on behalf of the Church, and as such must be publicly recognised and endorsed, but it has its roots in *charism*. Ministry is the public and communally recognised form of *charism*. This was well expressed by Bernard Cook in his encyclopaedic study of ministry:

> Ministerial rôle is the expression of *charism*. Not only such manifestly '*charismatic*' activities as prophecy are rooted in this empowering by the Spirit, but also regularised teaching and structured governing. This means that one cannot simply contrast '*charism*' and 'institution' in the life of the Church. Institutions themselves are meant to be the organs through which the Spirit-animated community expresses its life.[80]

This reinforces an earlier point about the relation of ecclesial ministry to Jesus' ministry of the Kingdom. Although *charisms* serve the ministry of the Church, they are also signs of the promised Kingdom. They not only build up the body of Christ but also point to the coming reign of God:

> And it shall come to pass afterward, that I will pour out my spirit on all flesh; your sons and your daughters shall prophesy, your old men shall dream dreams, and your young men shall see visions (Joel 2: 28).

In part the tendency to isolate *charisms* from the regular ministerial life of the Church arises from a misleading separation of the work of Christ from that of the Spirit. While the Spirit comes as gift to individual Christians he also comes, like the Son, as the manifestation of God's promise to reconcile all things to himself. In this sense the ministerial church is both 'in Christ' and 'in the Spirit'. In celebrating and proclaiming the coming of Christ and the Spirit the Church points to that final reign of God when he shall be 'all in all'. It would be as wrong, then, to divorce ministry from *charism* as it would be to divorce the somatic rôle of Christ from the ecstatic rôle of the Spirit. The Church, as sacrament of the Kingdom, is the creation of the Father through Christ and by the power of the Holy Spirit.

Ministry and the Church as Fulfilment

As a constitutive element in the life of the Church, ministry represents the Church not only as sign or promise but also its other sacramental dialectic as fulfilment.[81] Functionalist theologies of ministry are incomplete for they address the question of the Church only under its aspect of sign and promise. The Church and its ministry has to do not only with the means of salvation but also its end. We have already hinted at this when speaking of the ministry of proclamation. When the Church proclaims the gospel of the Kingdom it points to the promised Kingdom but also, in an important sense, anticipates that same Kingdom's fulfilment. Those who, in faith, preach the message are already gifted by the Holy Spirit and in this sense already taste the final fruit of salvation.

In his ministry Jesus is sent by the Father in the power of
the Holy Spirit. This does not betoken a subordination of the
Son to the Spirit but rather reflects the fact that Jesus'
coming is with power, the power of the end-time itself. Jesus
speaks as 'one having authority' because his ministry is
self-evidently a manifestation of God's Spirit at work. The
importance of the Spirit in this context is, of course, that he
is the 'guarantee of our inheritance' (Ephesians 1: 14). Just
as we have spoken of Christ as the 'Kingdom in person' so
we might describe the Holy Spirit as the 'hope of all things
in person'. The Holy Spirit is the gift of the glorified Christ
(John 7: 39). He it is who comes as the Pentecostal gift, not
only reminding the disciples of all that Jesus said, but also
declaring the 'things that are to come' (John 16: 13). It is this
that led St Symeon the New Theologian to praise the Holy
Spirit as the *eschaton* in person: 'Come, eternal life . . . come,
hope which will save all. Come, resurrection of the dead;
come, O powerful one, who fulfillest, transformest and
changest all things by thy will alone . . .'[82] The Church is the
community of those to whom God in Christ has revealed his
plan for the fullness of time 'to unite all things in him'
(Ephesians 1: 10). But the Church is not merely the bearer
of this message; it is already, even in this age, 'sealed with
the promised Holy Spirit' (Ephesians 1: 13). The Church
and its ministry, as the body of Christ, is already a manifestation of Christ as 'the fullness of him who fills all in all'
(Ephesians 1: 23).

We must be careful, then, to resist the temptation to speak
of the Church's ministry only in terms of the incarnation.[83]
Indeed it is unhelpful to speak of the Church as an extension
of the incarnation for it is also the recipient of the Pentecostal
gift. The Church and its ministry is not only *anamnesis* of the
life and death of Christ, it is also *epiclesis*, a manifestation and
celebration of the Pentecostal gift of the risen and glorified
Christ. Ministry, in other words, has its roots not only in
christology but also in pneumatology. In its ministry of proclamation the Church speaks of the past only in terms of the

future. In speaking of Christ it speaks of the one who has come and who is to come.

Notes

1. James M. Barnett, *The Diaconate A Full and Equal Order* (New York, 1979), pp. 3–10, 31, 96, 100, 104, 106, 111–112.
2. See, for example, the helpful discussion of the scale of the problem in Kenan B. Osborne, *Ministry: Lay Ministry in the Roman Catholic Church, Its History and Theology* (New Jersey, 1993).
3. Helen Oppenheimer, 'Ministry and Priesthood' in Eric James (ed.) *Stewards of the Mysteries of God* (London, 1979), p. 12.
4. ibid.
5. ibid.
6. John N. Collins, *Diakonia: Re-interpreting the Ancient Sources* (Oxford, 1990).
7. *Theologisches Wörterbuch zum Neuen Testament*, ed. G. Kittel, 2 (1935), pp. 81–93; Eng. trans., *Theological Dictionary of the New Testament*, 2 (1964), pp. 81–93.
8. Dieter Georgi, *The Opponents of Paul in Second Corinthians* (Philadelphia, 1986), pp. 27–32.
9. Edward Schweizer, *Church Order in the New Testament* (London, 1961), pp. 173–78; C.F.D. Moule, 'Deacons in the New Testament', *Theology*, lviii no. 425 (1955), p. 405; see also H. Lietzmann, *A History of the Early Church*, Vol. 1 (London, 1961), p. 145.
10. John N. Collins, op. cit. p. 194.
11. ibid., p. 251.
12. Although Collins's literary and historical scholarship is undoubtedly impeccable, his work is not without its problems. While he disclaims any theological or ecclesiological concerns one cannot help discerning a sub-text at play in his study. In his 'Afterword' (pp. 253–263), where he spells out very briefly some of the implications of his word study, we are invited to contemplate the abandonment of anything approaching a sacerdotal interpretation of ordained ministry. At the same time the book leaves it unclear whether or not ministry, in Collins's sense of the term, is open to both lay and ordained. While he is clear that 'ministry' is not a general or universal characteristic of the Christian life, Collins sometimes suggests that it should be restricted to the ordained, and at other times

that it should be applied to the gifts granted to both the laity and the clergy.

13. See, for example, Avery Dulles, *Models of the Church* (New York, 1978), pp. 105–6 and *The Resilient Church* (New York, 1977), p. 17.

14. Even though he makes use of the discredited interpretation of *diakonia* as servanthood, Thomas Franklin O'Meara, *Theology of Ministry* (New York, 1983), p. 3, also defines ministry as 'action on behalf of the community'.

15. ibid., p. 159.

16. For a detailed discussion of this, see Yves M.J. Congar, *Lay People in the Church* (London, 1957), pp. 22–52.

17. cf. also Matt. 4: 12–17; 4: 23; 9: 35; Lk. 4: 43; 8: 1; 9:11.

18. For a discussion of the question of the authenticity of the synoptists' account of Jesus' teaching see, for example, G.E. Ladd, *The New Testament and Criticism* (Grand Rapids, 1967), and 'The Search for Perspectives', *Interpretation*, XXV (1971), pp. 41–62.

19. For the theologian and the exegete the question of whether or not it is legitimate to speak of a divine plan occurs at two levels. First, there is the exegetical question of how far the New Testament writers' work is premised on the idea of promise and fulfilment. Secondly, there is the wider question of how far it is legitimate to speak of a biblical theology, that is, of a sacred history or a divine plan which is reflected in the text of scripture.

20. cf. Ps. 91: 1; 96: 10; 97: 1; 99: 1; 47: 6–9; 145: 13; Ex. 15: 18; Num. 23: 21; Isa. 6: 5; 43: 15; 2 Kings 19: 15; Jer. 46: 18.

21. For a discussion of this see Norman Perrin, *Jesus and the Language of the Kingdom: Symbol and Metaphor in New Testament Interpretation* (Philadelphia & London, 1976), pp. 16–32.

22. For a comprehensive discussion of this see G.E. Ladd, *The Presence of the Future: The Eschatology of Biblical Realism* (London, 1980).

23. Karl Barth, *The Epistle to the Romans* (London, 1933), p. 498.

24. Walter Kasper, *Jesus the Christ* (Tunbridge Wells, 1976), p. 187.

25. ibid., p. 77.

26. An expression quoted favourably by the modern Catholic theologian Thomas Franklin O'Meara, op. cit., p. 27.

27. G. E. Ladd, op. cit., p. 3.

28. Gunther Bornkamm, *Jesus of Nazareth* (New York, 1960), p. 200.

29. ibid., pp. 169f; cf. Ladd, op. cit., p. 35.

30. cf. Col. 1: 15–19.

31. W. Kasper, op. cit., p. 186; cf. Gal. 4: 4.

32. Origen, 'In Matth. tom. xiv, 7', *GCS*, vol. 40, p. 289.
33. L.S. Thornton, *The Incarnate Lord. An Essay concerning the Doctrine of the Incarnation in its relation to Organic Conceptions* (London, 1928), p. 168.
34. W. Kasper, op. cit., p. 101.
35. It can be argued that it is such an identification that ultimately lies behind absolutist views of ministry. See the discussion of juridical absolutism in Yves Congar's *Jesus Christ* (London, 1968), p. 156f.
36. *Didache* 10: 5.
37. Augustine, *The City of God*, XX 6–10.
38. Congar, *Lay People in the Church*, p. 59.
39. ibid.
40. ibid.
41. ibid., p. 59 f.
42. Matthew's version of this passage, 24: 14, makes it clear that this is the good news about the Kingdom.
43. C.E.B. Cranfield, *The Gospel According to St Mark* (Cambridge, 1959), p. 399.
44. The Orthodox theologian John D. Zizioulas, *Being As Communion. Studies in Personhood and the Church* (New York, 1985), p. 211, has been particularly critical about what he terms historicism in ecclesiology. In his view the Church's ministry ought not to be conceived in salvation-historical terms as existing in an interim period, awaiting the final accomplishment of the Kingdom. Rather he argues that it 'exists as an expression of the *totality* of the Economy'. The Church's ministry involves not simply a remembrance of the past or a service to the needs of the present, it is also a feature of the future as well 'sustaining for creation the hope of the *eschata*, of sharing God's very life, by offering a *taste* of that here and now'(ibid.).
45. G. E. Ladd, op. cit., p. 268.
46. See K.E. Skydsgaard's discussion of this theme in 'Kingdom of God and church', *Scottish Journal of Theology*, IV (1951), pp. 383–397.
47. For a discussion of the unity in distinctiveness of Christ and the Church see Yves Congar, *Jesus Christ*, pp. 156 ff.
48. A.T. and R.P.C. Hanson, *The Identity of the Church: A Guide to Recognising the Contemporary Church* (London, 1987), p. ix.
49. While the sacramental model of the Church has not received much attention outside Catholic circles there is a constructive discussion of it by the Protestant theologian Eberhard Jungel. See his 'The Church as Sacrament?' in *Eberhard Jungel: Theological Essays*, Eng. tr. J.B. Webster (Edinburgh, 1989),

pp. 189–213. The model was also used by the Anglican theologian H. Burn-Murdoch in *Church, Continuity and Unity* (Cambridge, 1945), pp. 31–37.

50. Henri de Lubac, *Catholicism* (London, 1950), p. 29.
51. Karl Rahner, *The Church and the Sacraments* (London, 1974). cf. his 'Membership of the Church according to the teaching of Pius XII's Encyclical *Mystici Corporis Christi*' in *Theological Investigations*, Vol 2 (London, 1963) pp. 1–88.
52. See Karl Rahner, *Foundations of Christian Faith* (New York, 1978), pp. 411–13.
53. E. Jungel, op. cit., p. 191
54. Walter Kasper, 'The Church as a Universal Sacrament of Salvation' in *Theology and Church* (London, 1989), p. 119.
55. *Lumen Gentium* 5.
56. *Lumen Gentium* 1.
57. K. Rahner, *The Church and the Sacraments*, p. 18.
58. ibid., p. 21.
59. In a memorable passage John Zizioulas, op.cit., p. 180, describes the Eucharist as 'the memory of the future'.
60. Karl Rahner, op. cit., p. 19.
61. J. D. Zizioulas, op. cit., p. 217 n. 20.
62. ibid., p. 215f; see also his 'Some Reflections on Baptism, Confirmation and Eucharist' in *Sobornost*, 5 (1969), pp. 644–652.
63. See J. Zizioulas, op.cit., p. 216.
64. Kenan B. Osborne, op. cit., pp. 48–113.
65. T. F. O'Meara, op. cit., p. 157.
66. ibid., p. 158.
67. See Henri de Lubac, *The Splendour of the Church* (New York, 1956), pp. 85–125.
68. ibid., p. 102.
69. ibid.
70. It is appropriate here to raise the question of the ecclesiological significance of Jesus' teaching about greatness in the Kingdom: 'If anyone wants to be first, he must make himself last of all and servant of all' (Mark 9: 35). The visible ordering of ecclesial life is in itself an aspect of the Church's proclamation of the Kingdom.
71. Henri de Lubac, op. cit., p. 103.
72. ibid.
73. Augustine, *Contra Faustum*, bk. xii, ch. xvi: '*Ex omnibus gentibus multitudinem congregat Ecclesia*'; '*Ecclesia corpus Christi in unitatem collecta*'. [PL, 42, 263].
74. Henri de Lubac, op. cit., p. 105.

75. ibid. p. 110 f.
76. The work of the Protestant church historian and theologian Adolf von Harnack at the beginning of the century played a decisive rôle in shaping this interpretation. cf. Adolf von Harnack, *The Constitution and Law of the Church* (New York, 1910), p. 236.
77. T. F. O'Meara, op. cit., p. 61.
78. E. Käsemann, 'Ministry and Community in the New Testament', in *Essays on New Testament Themes* (Napierville, 1964), p. 73.
79. T. F. O'Meara, op. cit., p. 61.
80. B. Cooke, *Ministry in Word and Sacrament* (Grand Rapids, 1976), p. 198.
81. The successful identification of the Church and its ministry after the pattern of the Kingdom's fulfilment is obviously a complex matter, requiring a careful balancing of the two aspects of the Church. In his groundbreaking work on the eucharistic identity of the Church John Zizioulas has tried to achieve just such a balance by rejecting an ontological identification of the Church and Christ and conceiving the relationship in a way that is thoroughly eschatological. Zizioulas insists that in the Eucharist the Church is 'momentarily' taken up into the community of the age to come. Indeed, such is his sense of this, albeit momentary, identification that Zizioulas can say that 'there is no room for the slightest distinction between the worshipping eucharistic community on earth and the actual worship in front of God's throne'. J. Zizioulas, op. cit., p. 233.

In his recent comparison of the ecclesiologies of de Lubac and Zizioulas Paul McPartlan illustrates the significant differences between the two theologians on this point. De Lubac, while consistently portraying Christ as distinct from the Church, even the Church in heaven, nonetheless describes the *eschaton* as *continuously* present in time. Zizioulas, in contrast, conceives its presence in terms of *visitation*. As McPartlan himself puts it: 'The thrust of Zizioulas's "strong eschatological emphasis" is not to make an abiding identification between the pilgrim church of sinners and the church of heaven, but rather to make the *momentary* identification of the earthly community around the bishop with the heavenly church around Christ'. Paul McPartlan, *The Eucharist Makes the Church*, (Edinburgh) p. 266.

In Zizioulas's view the Church in this age never completely attains the *eschaton* so as to keep it. The identification of the church on earth with Christ should not, in his view, be conceived ontologically but rhythmically. The Christian Church moves from foretaste to foretaste, constantly acquiring that which is also lost again and again. Zizioulas's view on this matter is entirely consistent with his refusal to contemplate the absorption of either the *eschaton* or the Holy Spirit into history. Although Zizioulas identifies the Eucharist with Pentecost he refuses to see this as a permanent presence. As McPartlan puts it, for Zizioulas 'The Spirit does not abide in the church from the past, but rather breaks upon her historical life from the future'. Paul McPartlan, op. cit., p. 220. In other words, the *eschaton* cannot be understood as 'the result of historical process as the climax of mission' but only as 'a presence from beyond history'. J. Zizioulas, op. cit., p. 174. The Church cannot be understood as permanently embodying the *eschaton* for the *eschaton* is not within history but beyond it.

While Zizioulas's defence of the eschatological dimension of the Church is both intriguing and illuminating there are serious problems with it. Notwithstanding McPartlan's insistence that Zizioulas's ideas reflect a dialectic between the earthly church and the heavenly church gathered around Christ, the eucharistic community on earth — albeit momentarily — is said to be absolutely identified with Christ in his fullness. Paul McPartlan, op. cit., p. 284. At this point of 'visitation' the eucharistic community quite literally becomes the eschatological community. Zizioulas has been careful to insist that God's freedom is absolute, and that the incarnation cannot be said to lend an inevitability to God's presence in the Church. Indeed it is precisely this that led to his great stress on eschatology and the Holy Spirit. Even in the incarnation God remains sovereign and free since the eschatological God cannot be enclosed in history. Otherwise, in Zizioulas's view, the *eschaton* rather than determining history is captured by it. It is this that leads Zizioulas to insist that the Church exists only from the future. The Church exists epicletically, and this shows that 'there is no security for her to be found in any historical guarantee as such — be it ministry or word or sacrament or even the historical Christ Himself. Her constant dependence on the Spirit proves that her history is to be constantly eschatological.' J. Zizioulas, op. cit., p. 185 f. Zizioulas's argument at this point illustrates the difficulty created by failing to observe the dialectical nature of the Church's experience of promise and fulfilment. His collapse of the dialectic at that point of visitation where the future encounters the Church in the Eucharist, is as much an intrusion upon the divine freedom and transcendence as the incarnational inevitabilism from which he was so careful to distance himself.

82. PG cxx., 507–9.
83. See Joseph Ratzinger, *Introduction to Christianity* (New York, 1979), pp. 256 ff., for a discussion of the implications of the failure to address ecclesiology from a pneumatological perspective.

3

Order and Ministry in the Social Pattern of the New Testament Church

Brian J. Capper

In the authentic letters of Paul, the earliest set of Christian sources, 'ministry' (*diakonia*) is not the preserve of the leading officers of the congregation, but the service which the Spirit inspires in each believer: 'There are varieties of gifts, but the same Spirit; varieties of service ('ministerings', *diakoniōn*), but the same Lord; and there are varieties of working ('energisings', *energēmatōn*), but it is the same God who inspires them all in every one' (1 Cor. 12: 4–6). 'Ministry' is the working of the Spirit through each believer for the common good (1 Cor. 12: 7; 14: 4). All have a contribution to the edification of all (1 Cor. 14: 26; cf. Rom. 12: 3–8). Paul's vision of the Church as a mutually nourishing, charismatically inspired community, in which each believer as a member of Christ's body has an individual, Spirit-inspired contribution to make, practical, oracular, or miraculous, in the public context of worship, can hardly be reconciled with Ignatius of Antioch's conception of the Church in the early second century, in which the community's existence is defined by the threefold order of bishop, elders and deacons and in

61

which it is difficult to imagine the layperson having a prominent place or public rôle at all. The bishop's central rôle in
instruction, in conduct of the liturgy, in baptising, in control
of finances and in the settlement of matters of dispute, and
the presence around him of defined classes of officials (the
elders and deacons) who fill out the public activities of the
Church in teaching, assistance in the liturgy, and care for the
poor suggest a form of community in which a clergy class had
arrogated to itself all authority and public expression of the
gospel in acts of ministry.

The transition from the former state of affairs to the latter
is susceptible to easy sociological caricature as the closing
phase of a process of institutionalisation by which a group
comes to be defined by its bureaucracy, which governs principally for the preservation of its own status and the exclusion
of challenges to it. The bureacracy, in effect, becomes the
institution. This would, however, be to make an unduly
negative assessment of the rôle of the clergy in Ignatius'
time. At the stage beyond the death of the last apostles, it is
apparent that developments of doctrine were abroad which
threatened the community's unity and continuity with its
apostolic roots and tradition. The Letters of John in the New
Testament, from the immediately preceding period, clearly
reveal a context in which stalk the spectres of incipient
Gnosticism and openly docetic christology, against which
Christian teachers had to take a stand to preserve an authentic version of Christianity for later generations. The danger
of the fragmentation of doctrine, and thence of the Christian
community itself, appeared with the passing of the apostolic
generation, whose natural authority while they were still
alive was largely able to keep in check doctrinal deviations.
'Ignatius connects the monarchical bishop with the preservation of the orthodox faith in such a way as to suggest that
a principal aim of monepiscopacy was to preserve right doctrine.'[1] The Church's struggle against Gnosticism in the
second century confirmed the necessity to gather around
those who preserved the apostolic tradition.

Ministry and the Social Scale of the Congregation

This paper proposes that the tendency for the exclusion of the 'laity' from 'ministry' was in significant measure an unintended consequence of the closer gathering of the Christian communities, by Ignatius' time very large and therefore less easy to defend, around the bishop as the preserver of apostolic tradition. It is frequently asserted that the struggle against heresy contributed to the development of monepiscopacy. It has not been observed, however, that the gathering of the church around the bishop brought changes in the social pattern of the Church from its earlier form in the New Testament period. By their very nature these changes diminished the opportunities for lay involvement in the public life and worship of the congregation. It is increasingly clear that the churches of the Pauline mission had what we might term today a 'cellular' structure, based on groups which were hosted by wealthier households. The church in each city was made up of a number of these house-groups, sponsored by prominent Christians whose own homes accommodated the worship of small groups of believers. In Romans 16: 3 a church meets in the house of Prisca and Aquila; another house-group is mentioned in Rom. 16: 5. In Romans 16: 10–11 groups are identified from the households of Aristobulus and Narcissus. Wayne Meeks finds in the three lists of names in Rom. 16: 14–15 three further household groups.[2] At Corinth groups of believers appear to have met in the households of Crispus, converted with his whole household, whose former rôle as synagogue-ruler also confirms his householder status (Acts 18: 5–8), and Gaius, who was a host to Paul and to 'the whole church' when Paul wrote to Rome from Corinth (Rom. 16: 23). Gaius probably had the largest premises, and so could entertain all the Christians at Corinth, although smaller gatherings in other houses also took place. Stephanas appears also to have hosted a group (1 Cor. 16: 19). At Laodicea, the householder Nympha entertained a church in her house (Col. 4: 15).

How large were these early household groups? The physical dimensions of excavated houses of the first century help us with this question. At Pompeii and Herculaneum many larger houses of the wealthy classes were well preserved by volcanic ash and lava in AD 79. At Herculaneum, the dimensions of the atrium or principal room of such houses average about twenty-five by thirty feet; the courtyards, when found in such houses, average about thirty-three by fifty feet. At Pompeii the atria average about thirty-one by forty-two feet and the peristyle courtyards fifty-five by sixty-seven feet.[3] Thus the atrium of a house could give protected meeting-space for maximally two or three dozen people (less to be comfortable, especially at the meal[4]); courtyards could accommodate one or two hundred, weather permitting. These physical dimensions suggest two types of early Christian gatherings. The Christian community in a city will normally have met in groups of two dozen or so within its larger households. Occasionally all within the city will have gathered together in the courtyard of a grander house to hear major visitors or for major deliberations, conditions permitting.

The principal act of Christian worship in the churches of the Pauline mission was clearly the taking together of a meal which included ritual actions (1 Cor. 11: 17–34). Later Christianity saw the eucharist as the defining act of Christian worship, confirming the priority in earlier times of the smaller household gathering over the larger, more occasional meeting. These meals did not take place in the early decades in cult-centres analogous to the meal-rooms of the Graeco-Roman clubs, but privately in larger households. Whether the meal-fellowship was comfortable or cramped, the number attending can rarely have been more than two or three dozen.

It is apparent that Paul's vision of the 'ministry' of all believers can really only be realised in such circumstances, when the meeting of the Christian congregation is relatively small. Every individual cannot make meaningfully frequent contribution to the worship of a group which exceeds two or three dozen. Paul's vision of the Church as a charismatic community, therefore, is a vision based on the assumption that Christians meet in relatively small groups, in which all from the least to the greatest can make regular contribution.

Paul applies the metaphor of the body to the congregation; as the various parts of a human body differ in function but are each necessary to the life of the whole, so the contribution of the humblest service to congregational life is as necessary as even the most spectacular gift. Paul emphasises that the Spirit works through every member of the congregation (1 Cor. 12: 5) and gives examples of inspired workings of the Spirit through each individual (vv. 8–10). Paul's later re-use of the example of prophecy emphasises that all may minister through the Spirit; he encourages all to prophesy (14: 1, 5), and envisages situations when this will happen (v. 24). The capacity of all to prophesy is probably explained at 14: 26, where at the coming together of Christians for worship 'each one has a hymn, a lesson, a revelation, a tongue, or an interpretation'. This letter gives us the earliest account which we possess of the form of Christian worship. The eucharist (1 Cor. 11: 17–34), conducted in the context of a meal within a household, must be augmented with the worship pattern delineated in chapters 12 to 14, in which each member of the congregation makes individual contribution, to form a full impression of what happened in earliest Christian worship. Paul can only have presented this understanding of Christian life and worship on the assumption that the churches throughout his mission usually met in small, household groups, whose members might reasonably *all* have been encouraged to prophesy or relay the contribution of the Spirit through them in other ways, including practical service, to the meeting. We know that from earliest times Christians had broken bread 'from house to house' (Acts 2: 46). From Romans 12: 8 it is clear that Paul counted practical acts of service amongst the *charismata*.

By the time of Ignatius, Christian worship was taking place on an altogether larger scale. Ignatius depicts the bishop presiding over the eucharist, surrounded by his council of elders, and assisted in his ministry to the gathered laity by numerous deacons.[5] Thus, the clergy themselves of a meeting of Ignatius' congregation may have outnumbered the typical house-church of earlier times. We are dealing with typical Christian meetings not of two or three dozen, but perhaps of two or three hundred souls or more. The scale of these meetings may imply that the gathering of large groups of believers, which as we have seen was probably only occasional in earlier times, had now become the normal pattern of events. Protected physical facilities were certainly now available to allow much larger meetings to occur at all times of the year, regardless of the weather or season. It may be that the scale of these gatherings has to do with the sheer success of the Christian mission and the number of believers in each city. In regard to what we have said above about the emphasis on the bishop as the bearer of the apostolic tradition and bulwark against heresy, however, it is apparent that the scale of these meetings may also have been a product of the conflicts of the age. Believers were gathered into larger groups to hearken to the secure voice of apostolic tradition, rather than remain is smaller house-congregations with separate eucharists. This development probably happened because the meeting of smaller and more independent sub-groups in the congregation would be treated with suspicion because of the potential promulgation in them of heterodox teaching. All the believers in the locality were gathered week by week around the bishop for the sake of uniform adherence to the apostolic doctrine as conveyed by the bishop and the gathered elders.

The symbolic significance which Ignatius sees in the different officers of the congregation makes it plain that the situation which he describes marks a change from the pattern of Christian worship in earlier times. Ignatius makes the bishops, deacons and elders (given in this order) respectively images of God, Christ, and the apostles.[6] This is a very awkward ordering and analogy, since the deacons are made to rank above the elders, or worse (if the elements are rearranged in their expected order) the apostles to rank above Christ. The earlier form of the image is apparent on reflection. Originally it had been about the pair of offices of the meal president and the deacons who served the meal — pictures of God seated in majesty, and Christ humbly serving humanity through the meal which was his body. Two offices have become three by the time of Ignatius. Clearly elders appearing as a gathered council were a new social reality, and they were awkwardly appended to the image.

To anticipate some of the analysis of early Christian offices given below, it is apparent that the image in its earlier context related to the household meal-gathering, at which the host presided and trusted servants or others of the group served. The prominent householders who hosted the earlier household gatherings have now coalesced into a council of elders; the boundaries between individual house-churches within the city have now passed away; there is only one, larger congregation. Since the eucharist had always needed a presiding figure, above the resulting elder-council there now appears a prominent individual, perhaps formerly one of their number or a renowned local teacher or prophet, who takes charge of the meeting of the much larger group and takes over conduct of the eucharistic liturgy from the householder class.

It would be vain to hope that in the larger congregational form, the product both of successful evangelism and of the fight against doctrinal fragmentation, Paul's vision of meaningful participation by each member of the congregation could find expression. Already in earlier times, larger meetings had been different in character from the smaller household gatherings. In the household gathering of two dozen, Paul's vision that every believer had a contribution — a contribution of *ministry* — to make to the community could be realised in practice. In the smaller social context, the wisdom which each brought to the meeting could be heard, and the practical service which each rendered could be enjoyed by all. In the much larger congregations of Ignatius' day, this was not possible. In a gathering of several hundred souls, the bishop could preside, and one or two elders would speak. Deacons distributed the elements of the eucharist; practical tasks such as doorkeeping or reading might perhaps be allotted to others. But while the general encouragement of all Christians practically to serve each other could remain, the scale of the congregation's meeting meant that the ordinary believer's active participation in the public gathering was effectively excluded. History witnesses to the lively nature of the practical service which Christians rendered to each other outside the meeting, but such was taken from public view, and therefore, potentially, from the focus of the Church's self-understanding.

The adjustment which we have traced in the scale of the Christian meeting in fact helps us towards understanding where we may find in the New Testament period the roots of the threefold ministry of bishop, elder, and deacon which appears with Ignatius in the early second century. It is not without trepidation that we approach the question of the possible origins of the later offices (order) of the Christian church in the New Testament period. Many have maintained that 'office' is strictly incompatible with Paul's lively view of a church created by the *charismata* which the Spirit inspires.[7] Paul's exposition of the Body of Christ in 1 Cor. 12: 4–11 has been assumed by some to exclude the possibility of authority-bearing offices, of rank. Is not the only president of the congregation the inspiring Spirit, who himself guides the meeting? Is it not the Spirit's address to the congregation through inspired *charismata* that makes God's authority present? Does not Paul's exposition of Christian worship as the ministry of all through the Spirit exclude any possible line of demarcation between 'laity' and 'officers' of the congregation? The classical exposition of this approach was given by the late nineteenth-century German church historian Rudoph Sohm, who sought, by sponsoring an anti-institutional view of the Church, to reincarnate the vigour of primitive Christianity.[8]

Such views probably misread Paul's purpose in this passage. He emphasises the complementarity of the Spirit's diverse 'energisings' in order to eradicate the damaging cleavage caused by false and self-vaunting interest in the more spectacular gifts, and his focus is drawn first to his opponents' ground, the spectacular *charismata*. After he has followed through his point that different gifts of the Spirit must complement rather than compete with each other (1 Cor. 12: 12–26), he presents a second list of the Spirit's workings in which appear both *practical service* and *office*. The language of official, hierarchical structure forcefully emerges: 'And God has *appointed* in the church *first* apostles, *second* prophets, *third* teachers . . .' (12: 28). The proper working of the Spirit through all is not furthered by the absence of government. The vehemence with which Paul elsewhere defends his own authority as an apostle shows that his intent is hardly likely to be spiritual anarchy. He opposes not the proper boundaries of office, but merely the false barriers constructed on the basis of the foolish vaunting of the more spectacular *charismata*.

With mention of the 'teachers', the numbering of the sequence of 1 Cor. 12: 28 ceases, each element thereafter being introduced with simply 'then . . . then . . .' (*epeita . . . epeita . . .*), implying that what follows does not bear authority comparable with the first three offices. Comparison of the sequence of inspired workings of the Spirit which follow with those of Paul's first list is informative. Glossolalia, working of miracles and healing are repeated from the first list; 'faith' and 'discerning of spirits' are omitted. The 'word of knowledge' and 'word of wisdom' of the first list (12: 8) have no equivalent in the second. Paul may already have covered this area of the Spirit's working in his reference to the prophets of the Christian church; in any event, it is clear that the list is illustrative rather than exhaustive. Although in 1 Cor. 12: 3–8 Paul seems to limit the workings of the Spirit, which he understands as 'ministry', to inspired speech and various miraculous manifestations, in 1 Cor. 12: 28 more practical services are understood to be inspired by the Spirit: 'helpers' (*antilēmpseis*) and 'administrators' (RSV). This latter term, *kybernēseis*, which the King James Version memorably renders 'governments', is literally 'pilotings', and seems to indicate the rôle of leading worship. The 'helpers' and 'administrators' seem to indicate nascent offices in the local congregation. If the 'administrators' preside at the community gathering, directing the affairs of worship, the term probably

indicates the leading householders. The 'helpers' are probably their assistants, where assistance was required, in the
arrangements for and serving of the meal, and perhaps in the
administering of associated charity. The pair of terms may
anticipate the later offices of 'deacon' and 'bishop'. Although
Paul remains in rhetorical vein, his second list comes closer
to being an actual description of the congregation as it
functioned in his time. Certainly, the working of the Spirit
issues in (rather than excludes) the presence of established
offices.

Most would agree, however, that Paul's churches at the
time when he wrote his letters contained only nascent institutional structure. References to those who seem to carry
authority are infrequent, and terminology fluid. We should
not expect to find substantial emphasis on local 'officials'
since these communities were young and, therefore, a pronounced transfer of authority from the apostle to local officers had not yet taken place. For these freshly founded
churches the travelling missionaries represent the greater
authority; that is why these letters were written. The remaining evidence for nascent authority-bearing offices in
Paul's letters is as follows. Paul refers in his first letter to
Thessalonica (AD 50/51), possibly the earliest New Testament writing,[9] within months of the founding of the church,
to those who 'are over' the congregation (*proïstamenoi*,
1 Thess. 5: 12). These may be local officers, equivalent to
the 'helpers' and 'administrators' of 1 Cor. 12: 28 whom Paul
mentions some four years later. Within a further year or two,
Paul addresses the 'overseers' (*episkopoi*, 'bishops') and 'servants' (*diakonoi*, 'deacons') of the church at Philippi (Phil. 1: 1).
In his letter to Rome (*c.* AD 56, although we do not know
when the church was founded) Paul mentions Phoebe the
'servant' (*diakonos*, possibly 'deacon') of the church at
Cenchreae (the port of Corinth). In his exposition of the
body of Christ in Romans 12: 3–8 he refers again, between
'he who contributes' (*metadidous*) and 'he who does acts of
mercy' (*eleōn*, perhaps the 'helper' of 1 Cor. 12: 28) to the
proïstamenos, translated in the New English Bible as 'leader',

though the Revised Standard Version renders 'he who gives aid'. Some think the 'prophets and teachers' who follow the 'apostles' in precedence in 1 Cor. 12: 28 may be local leaders rather than mobile missionaries, though we shall see below that this is less likely. These references come from the period of the first six or seven years of Paul's mission in Europe. With the exception of Rome, which Paul had not yet even visited, we know these churches were recently founded and still closely dependent upon Paul's own authority. While this is the sum of what the authentic Pauline correspondence has to say about local church officers, the relative youthfulness of these churches means that the paucity of evidence should not be taken to show that Paul had given no warrant for local organisational structure at all.

Can we detect a pattern of local organisation? We are certainly not dealing with offices so settled as to have a completely fixed terminology, although some terms appear more than once. None of these texts implies that a single individual was in charge of the church in any one city, and all can be taken to imply a plurality of local leaders. The monarchical episcopate as reflected in Christian writing from Ignatius of Antioch onwards (after AD 115) has no clear precedent in the *episkopos* of the New Testament. In Philippians 1: 1 the term *episkopos* appears in the plural (*episkopoi*), suggesting a plurality of 'overseers' in the one city of Philippi, seemingly something like a leadership class of elders (we cannot assume already a council). In Acts 14: 23, about two years prior to the founding of the church at Philippi, Paul and Barnabas are said to have chosen 'elders' in each church founded in southern Turkey on Paul's first missionary journey; thus these two texts seem to describe the same local institution of a plural leadership installed by the apostles.

Although the term *presbyteros* never appears in the authentic Pauline letters, the term 'overseer' ('bishop', *episkopos*) and 'elder' (*presbyteros*) seem to have been largely interchangeable for most of the first century. In Acts Paul addresses the 'elders' (Acts 20: 17, cf. 14: 23) at Ephesus as 'overseers' (v. 28). In Titus 1: 5–7 the command to Titus to appoint 'elders' is followed by a list of the qualifications desirable in the person designated *episkopos*. In 1 Peter 5: 1–2 'elders' are urged 'to exercise oversight', *episkopein* (the cognate verb). Clement of Rome passes from speaking of 'dissensions over the office of bishop' (*episkopos*), and the offence of removing the 'bishopric' or 'oversight' (*episkopē*) from those who rightfully exercise it, to speak of the blessedness of 'elders' (*presbyteroi*) who have died after faithfully serving in their office (1 Clement 44). The people in charge in 1 Thess. 5: 12 can be taken to be such 'presbyter-bishops' or 'elder-bishops', as can the 'administrators' of 1 Cor. 12: 28 and those who 'lead' (*proïstamenos*) in Romans 12: 8. There existed in the early Pauline congregations a plurality of leaders whom Paul variously acknowledged as 'leading' (*proïstamenos*), as 'overseers' ('bishops', *episkopoi*) or as 'administrators' (*kybernēseis*), whom the author of Acts calls both 'elders' (*presbyteroi*) and 'overseers' ('bishops' *episkopoi*).

It is regularly assumed that in the possession of a plural leadership of 'elders' the Christian Church from earliest times simply imitated the organisation of the synagogue. Indeed, J.T. Burtchaell has recently written at length on the rise of the pattern of the Church's officers, arguing that the synagogue is the model at every point.[10] His monograph is the most substantial attempt for many years at solving the problem of the rise of the 'threefold ministry' of bishops, elders and deacons which is universal by the middle of the second century. His hypothesis is simple. After the period of the Church's establishment, in which authority was wielded by the apostolic missionaries and other exceptional charismatic individuals, the Church settled down to a pattern based on the synagogue. Jewish synagogue worship was led by the 'ruler of the synagogue' (*archisynagōgos*), a single leader; eventually, local Christian congregations came to be overseen by a single community chief. Local Jewish communities acknowledged the jurisdiction of senior men usually called 'rulers' (*archontes*). The Christian bishop presided in the council of his elders (*presbyteroi*). In Christian worship the bishop was assisted at the meal by his deacons; the Jewish synagogue-ruler had a servant assistant (the *hypēretēs*).

However, the rise of the threefold ministry cannot be explained so simply. At all points the usual terminology for the Jewish office differs from its supposed Christian counterpart. The Christian designation *episkopos* for the leader of the community does not suggest a derivation from the synagogue. The assistant of the synagogue was never called *diakonos* in Greek.[11] The Diaspora evidence rarely suggests that the 'rulers' may have been called 'elders'.[12] Burthchaell is well aware of the acute difficulty which differing terminology makes for his proposal, but seeks to overcome it by stressing both the need for a model available to all the Christian congregations across the whole of the Mediterranean and the plausibility of the synagogue analogue in terms of overall social structure. The correspondence of social pattern is, however, as weak as the correspondence of terminology. In Christian worship the 'elders' play a prominent part, but the 'rulers' of the synagogue play no rôle in worship, constituting rather the judicial authority in the ethnic group. The Christian bishop is always assisted by a number of deacons, but the synagogue analogue offers, most problematically, only a single assistant. That the social pattern of the synagogue offices does not give broad correspondence with the pattern of the Christian Church only serves to emphasise the terminological divergence.[13]

The Threefold Ministry and the Social Pattern of the Early Churches

If the synagogue was not the pattern for the threefold ministry, how are we to proceed? We should look not outside early Christianity to understand the pattern of Christian order, but rather inward to its own characteristic social structures. The threefold ministry in fact arises out of social dimensions of early Christianity which are well-known and easily demonstrable from the New Testament text. The principal social realities of early Christianity were the peripatetic missionaries, the local meetings at which these were received within the household setting of wealthier members of the congregation, and the central act of a common meal, embracing ritual elements and care for the poor. In these social realities the grounds for the emergence of three classes of community officers are apparent. First, the early Christian churches were founded and re-visited by an acknowledged class of authoritative leaders who were *mobile missionaries dependent upon the congregations for their upkeep*. This group contained those originally called apostles, some of whom gained this title from a direct commission from the historical Jesus to preach, and others of whom seem to have acquired the title in virtue of their acknowledged gifts (e.g. James the brother of the Lord in Jerusalem) or in virtue of a commission to act as missionaries sponsored by particular congregations (2 Cor. 8: 23). Second, a plurality of local leaders, as outlined above, existed because they were *the early prominent converts who offered their households as the meeting places of the churches* and held authority in those gatherings in view of their seniority in the faith and their natural authority as hosts over meetings (which included the Christian meal) held in their homes. Far from receiving payment for what they gave to the congregation, they rather gained prominence through their material patronage, through which the congregations could meet and flourish. Unlike the peripatetic class above them, these householder-overseers were not in the full-time service of the church. Third, the central act of worship in the household meetings of the early congregations was a meal, in the context of which the poor were also provided for. The functioning of a formal meal involved not only a host but also *a group of servants*. At the early Christian meals, certain Christians were honoured with this rôle of serving the congregation as meal-servers. The following will outline how these three classes of *visitors*, *householders*, and honorary *meal-servants* became the threefold order of bishop, elders and deacons.

Tenuous.

A Class of Peripatetic Ministers

Adolf von Harnack stressed the distinction between the peripatetic ministry of the 'apostles', 'prophets', and 'teachers' who gain prominence in 1 Cor. 12: 28, and local officers of the congregation.[14] He distinguished the apostles, prophets and teachers as charismatic officers, who were appointed by the Spirit alone to a ministry to the universal Church. Over against these he set the officers who were elected by the local congregations and whose authority did not extend beyond these congregations. His position was determined by the discovery of the 'Teaching (*Didachē*) of the Twelve Apostles' in 1883. This sub-apostolic work from the close of the first century revealed a class of peripatetics, of whom the terms apostles, prophets and teachers were used, though not as a definite triad as in 1 Cor. 12: 28. The document showed caution about this waning class, which was to be carefully tested before being allowed to live at the expense of the congregation when visiting, and urged the appointment of a local ministry of 'bishops and deacons', effectively as their replacements:

> Appoint therefore for yourselves bishops and deacons worthy of the Lord, men that are gentle and without covetousness and true and approved: for they also minister to you the ministry of the prophets and teachers. Therefore despise them not; for they are your honoured ones together with the prophets and teachers. (XV.1)

Harnack's desire to reserve the term 'charismatic' for the peripatetic church officers only was clearly overdone and has required correction. As we have seen above, intimations of nascent local offices are to be found in the Pauline listing of *charismata* in 1 Cor. 12: 28. However, his observation that we must view the triad of officers which opens Paul's list in 1 Cor. 12: 28 as peripatetics after the manner of those revealed in the *Didachē* should probably be allowed to stand.[15] The construction of the list certainly implies that Paul thought of them as together comprising a distinct group. In the following we shall see that there is a substantial amount of evidence that those called apostles, prophets and teachers operated as peripatetics in the early decades.

The peripatetic must be maintained by the congregation if he is to fulfil his ministry, since otherwise he has no regular means of support. The social boundary between the triad which opens the list of 1 Cor. 12: 28 and what follows is therefore the combination of full-time, peripatetic ministry and a right to upkeep from the congregation. These two factors mark off the class of peripatetics very distinctly in sociological terms from the remainder of the list, and explain why after them the process of numbering ends completely. By contrast, we have no evidence from sources from the time of Paul or earlier that a local officer of the congregation (e.g. those called *proïstamenoi, episkopoi,* or *kybernēseis*) had any right to support. In the New Testament, only one reference in the Pastoral Epistles, from the last quarter of the first century, speaks of local elders who probably have a right to material support (1 Tim. 5: 17).[16] Thus only in the late first century, beyond the Pauline period, do we hear of officers in the local congregation who have a right to material support. The *Didachē*, at the close of the first century, envisages prophets and teachers settling down in one location. Should they thus settle, they are worthy of support (XIII.1–2).

The right of the apostle to support from the congregation goes back to Jesus' commissioning of some of his disciples to preach. Those commissioned to preach were said to be 'sent' (*apostolos*). They had to renounce their worldly occupations in order to fulfil this commission, and therefore were given a right to support from the congregations (Matt. 9: 35–10: 16; Mk. 6: 6–11; Lk. 9: 1–5, 10: 1–12). Paul, unusually, abstained from this right to support, at least on occasion, but is emphatic that it was justly his (1 Cor. 9: 1–18) and refers its precedent, in the mission charges later recorded in the Gospels, as the Lord's *commanding* (v. 9). The apostle has a right 'to eat and drink' (at the expense of the congregation, v. 4), 'to refrain from working for a living' (v. 6) and even to travel with a Christian wife who is also supported thus (v. 5). When Paul refers to 'the other apostles and the brothers of

the Lord and Cephas' availing themselves of these rights
(v.5), he reveals a firmly established social pattern in early
Christianity.

Harnack's thesis that the prophets too were a wandering
class has lost general approval because some consider it plain
that there were 'prophets' who were local to congregations,
particularly since Paul envisaged that all at Corinth could
prophesy.[17] The strength of Harnack's view, however, cannot
be so easily overturned. Paul clearly distinguishes between
the office of a prophet and the fact that the prophetic Spirit
is available to all. His rhetorical questioning in 1 Cor. 12: 29
('Are all prophets?') stands in contrast to his general encouragement to all to prophesy (14: 5, 24, 31). If there were
'circles of prophets' in Corinth,[18] Paul does not have these in
mind in 1 Cor. 12: 28. The prophets whom he ranks second
in the order of the church are clearly to be distinguished from
the whole prophesying local congregation; they are figures in
whom the prophetic Spirit works with such power that they
gain second rank after the apostles.

The other key text in this debate is Acts 13: 1–3, where
we learn that 'in the church at Antioch prophets and teachers, Barnabas, Simeon who was called Niger, Lucius of
Cyrene, Mana'en a member of the court of Herod the tet-
rarch, and Saul'. This group receive the Lord's command
through prophecy while praying and worshipping together to
despatch Saul and Barnabas on their first missionary journey
in Asia Minor. Many take this reference to imply that the
group of 'prophets and teachers' were permanently settled
in the church at Antioch, but this is probably not the case.
They were probably based upon Antioch, but had a rôle of
travelling into the hinterland of Syria on preaching journeys
or to support newly founded congregations. Paul and
Barnabas themselves illustrate this possibility. Earlier,
Barnabas was sent from Jerusalem to observe the beginnings
of the gentile mission at Antioch (Acts 11: 22–24). Following
his investigation he fetched Paul from Tarsus to 'teach' at
Antioch for a year (vv. 25–26). Both had been despatched to
Jerusalem with aid for the church there (11: 29–30). However,

after such mobile services on behalf of the church, both are numbered amongst the 'prophets and teachers' at Antioch, rather than as apostles, in 13: 1. Following the reaping of converts for the faith in new areas, the Church had a system for establishing them in the faith by bringing in mobile teachers for lengthy stays, who would have the right of support from the new congregations. The special commission for the first missionary journey in Asia Minor (Acts 13: 2–3) seems to have been the basis for the term 'apostle' being thereafter applied to Paul and Barnabas in 14: 4 and 14. Prior to this calling, however, Paul and Barnabas were used to being despatched for special tasks as 'prophets and teachers'; so may have been all the group of Acts 13: 1. We see mobile prophets moving from Jerusalem to the church at Antioch in Acts 11: 27, presumably enjoying support. In Acts 15: 32 we see the prophets Judas and Silas ministering temporarily at Antioch, implicitly enjoying the support of the congregation, before moving on. There is little reason not to assume that the social patterns revealed in the *Didachē* do not apply to the prophets or teachers at Antioch in the early decades of the church. Certainly, missionary enterprise is the focus of interest where the 'prophets and teachers' of Antioch are mentioned in Acts 13: 1–3, as can be seen from the group's despatch of Saul and Barnabas.

The false prophets who have 'gone out into the world' at 1 Jn. 4: 1 probably expect the financial support of the congregations which they visit, and lead directly to the cautious words of the *Didachē* about providing for the visitor who claims to be an apostle or prophet.[19] Paul endorses the right of the 'teacher' to support from the congregation: 'Let him who is taught the word share all good things with him who teaches' (Gal. 6: 6). The 'prophets' who intervene between the apostles and the teachers in 1 Cor. 12: 28 cannot have been denied this right. They were individuals of outstanding *charisma* who could move from congregation to congregation enjoying the same kind of support as the apostles received; their near-apostolic status is confirmed in Eph. 2: 20, where they constitute with the apostles the foundation of the

Church. We learn of 'teachers' who were peripatetic in the *Didachē* in XI.1 and who should be 'received' if their doctrine is sound. In XIII.2 a 'true teacher' is worthy of his food, just as is 'every true prophet' in XIII.1 (cf. XI.10). The occasional fluidity of terminology between apostle, prophet and teacher in the *Didachē* is explained by the fact that what was common to individuals known by one of these titles was the right to upkeep from the congregation.

The Householders

The importance of the household structure for early congregations has not been drawn into the question of the origins of the threefold ministry. Rather, the preferred social patterns from which to build understanding have been the synagogue, or even the structure of the Graeco-Roman private religious associations.[20] It is, however, unlikely that these forms were significant at earliest times, because such patterns relate mainly to a public setting in which the religious group usually has a meeting-hall.[21] We learn that on one occasion Paul seems to have rented a room for teaching, the lecture hall of Tyrannus at Ephesus (Acts 19: 9), but his usual activity seems to have been in the private context of the households of his better-off converts. Until Christians began specially to adapt their meeting places towards the end of the first century (probably from private houses which had passed into the possession of the communities), it is unlikely that the patterns of the clubs and of the synagogue exerted any great influence. Until that development Christian believers met, as we have seen, within the household structure.[22] Christian households hosted and were coordinated by the travelling class of apostles, prophets and teachers.

The use of larger households for meetings naturally gave prominence to the householders who submitted their premises for use by the peripatetics and the congregations. Their hospitality and labour alongside the apostles and in their absence was a necessary condition for the creation of stable congregations. The authority which Paul in return vouchsafed

to those householders who helped maintain Christian congregations is apparent from the close of 1 Corinthians. At
16.15–16 he accords Stephanas and his house authority:

> Now, brethren, you know that the household of Stephanas
> were the first converts in Achaia, and they have devoted
> themselves to the service of the saints; I urge you be subject
> to such men and to every fellow-worker and labourer.

Paul accorded Stephanas and his household authority on the
grounds of their seniority in the faith, their obvious devotion,
and their suitability to the task. Since Paul remembered
baptising only Stephanas' household at Corinth (1 Cor. 1.16),
we can tell that their seniority in the faith had always given
them a prominent rôle. In Paul's eyes Stephanas could properly demand obedience from the congregation. Moreover,
Paul enjoins obedience not merely to Stephanas, but also to
'such men', i.e. to those who host particular groups of Christians within their homes. We have noted above that these
prominent householders included Crispus (Acts 18.5–8),
and Gaius (Rom. 16.23), who were seemingly the first and
second converted by Paul at Corinth.[23] There thus arose
under the guidance of the apostles a plurality of local leaders
who may be identified with the class of 'presbyter-bishops'
outlined above.

The deduction that Paul always invested such prominent
householders with authority may seem too much to read out
of a single verse in 1 Corinthians, but Clement of Rome,
writing in AD 96, a generation from these events, seems to
know that this verse actually gives the typical pattern by
which the apostles established local authority in the
churches. When writing later to Corinth, against those who
have deposed from authority the elders of the congregation,
he writes:

> Now, the Gospel was given to the Apostles for us by the Lord
> Jesus Christ; and Jesus the Christ was sent from God. That
> is to say, Christ received his commission from God, and the
> Apostles theirs from Christ. The order of these two events
> was according to the will of God. So thereafter, when the
> Apostles had been given their instructions, and all their

doubts had been set at rest by the resurrection of our Lord Jesus Christ from the dead, they set out in full assurance of the Holy Spirit to proclaim the coming of God's kingdom. And as they went through the territories and townships preaching, they appointed their first converts — after testing them by the Spirit — to be bishops and deacons for the believers of the future. (1 Clement 42)

It is possible that the Clement who wrote this was the contemporary of Paul of that name mentioned in Philippians 4: 3. Certainly, this passage seems to combine knowledge of 1 Corinthians 16: 15 (and 1: 16) with the phrase 'bishops and deacons' from Phil 1: 1. This section of 1 Clement is in fact the first exposition in Christian literature of the idea of apostolic succession.[24] Clement claims to know that this was a typical pattern in the early decades. He may have observed the process at first hand; what evidence we have supports his view.

Recent deductions concerning the social pattern of early Christianity dovetail with what Clement has to say. From the 'cellular' structure of the Pauline congregations which we have outlined above emerges the reason for the plurality of local leaders in each of the Pauline congregations. Each sub-group met within the house of a leader in the Christian community; each such leader is an elder-overseer, of which there was a plurality in each city. As we have deduced above, these gatherings were relatively small. Churches meeting in such a social pattern were dependent for their growth on the hospitality of certain wealthier community members. While grander houses could accommodate Christian meetings, the mean flats such as we observe at the port of Ostia, where poorer folk lived in very cramped conditions, could not.[25] Better-off, serious-minded believers opened their homes to others to provide a context for meal-fellowship, prayer, singing and teaching. Hospitality was itself in the ancient world a formal process with sacred overtones. In the modern world the significant intimacy extended through invitation into private households for meals commands deference to the hosts' views of the way events should proceed, and sometimes even to their political opinions. We can be certain that

in the ancient world the householder was vouchsafed ultimate control of any hosted gathering. This was custom and
common manners. Since early Christian householders who
entertained church meetings in their houses were always
older in the faith and the local sponsors of the gospel, they
became the commanding figures of the congregation at the
local level. Social status, maturity, generosity, *charisma* and
apostolic commission combined to give authority to these
local sponsors of the gospel. Gerd Theissen has studied the
information about individuals known to us by name at
Corinth and concludes that although there were not many
'wise, powerful, and well-born' at Corinth (1 Cor. 1: 26), it is
precisely this group who had prominence in the congregation.[26] He is aware of the theological issues which a link
between social position and gaining a position of power in
the church raises, and takes up E. Troeltsch's category of
'love-patriarchalism' to ease the difficulty: those in privi-
leged social position held power only through a trade in
which they placed their resources at the community's disposal.[27]

With this picture of the cellular social structure of Paul's
churches in mind, we may return to establish the precise
nuances of the references mentioned above to local leaders
in Thessalonica, Philippi, and Rome. The participle
proïstamenoi employed at 1 Thess. 5: 12 (RSV 'are over you')
comes from the verb *proïstemi* and may mean 'those who rule /
preside over you', 'those who are concerned about / care for
you', or 'those who stand before you as protectors / patrons'.[28]
In Paul's usage it probably combined all these elements. The
aspect of authority is clear from the subsequent participle
'admonishing' (*nouthetountes*), and the sense is certainly well-
attested for the verb in secular Greek and employed in
Jewish sources.[29] The preceding reference to labouring leads
into the nuance of care for the community.[30] The verb is used
in participial form of 'elders who have ruled well' at 1 Tim.
5: 17, which suggests a nuance of authority-bearing office.
We encounter here not care alone, but care from those who
are in a position of authority.

Several notable commentators see the technical nuance of 'patron' or 'protector' in the participle.[31] The feminine cognate noun *prostatis*, used of Phoebe's care for the church and for Paul himself in Rom. 16: 1–2, is well-attested with the technical sense of 'patroness'.[32] For Wayne Meeks the social context suggests the sense of 'patron' or 'protector' in 1 Thess. 5: 12, but the passage also implies both caring and 'some governing authority'.[33] A clue to the combination of nuances in the term is found in its other uses in connection with the offices of 'bishop' and 'deacon' in the Pastoral Epistles. It is *not* used of the rôle of these officers in the congregation, but of their ruling well within their households, as a necessary qualification for occupying these offices in the church (1 Tim. 3: 4, 5, 12). The term is only used in the Pastoral Epistles with respect to the rôle in the church of elders, in 1 Tim. 5: 17. For the elder, the church was quite simply an extension of his own household, for he hosted the church in his own home. Here we are at the heart of the matter. The head of a household has a position of authority (indeed of considerable authority[34]), is the provider for and carer for all within the household (family, slaves, and servants) and is through his social status and wealth the patron and protector of all. The early Pauline house-churches enjoyed the care and patronage of socially prominent local sponsors of the gospel, and also acknowledged their authority. These householder-patrons of the church became the class of presbyter-bishops discerned above, observable as a plurality of local leaders already in 1 Thess. 5: 12. As with the prominent householders at Corinth, Paul's elevation of this group to authority is apparent in his demand that the congregation at Thessalonica should 'esteem them very highly in love' (v. 13).

As noted above, the same participle appears in Paul's account in Romans 12: 3–8 (*ho proïstamenos*, v. 8) of the various 'members' (v. 4) of the body which is the Christian congregation. As we have noted, the New English Bible translates 'leader'[35] although the Revised Standard Version (inconsistent with its translation of 1 Thess 5: 12) renders 'he who gives aid'. Some argue that, since in the same verse the previous member in Paul's list is 'he who shares' (*ho metadidous*) and the subsequent member is 'he who does acts of mercy' (*ho eleōn*), we should see the intervening term as derivative from the verb *proïstēmi* in its alternative sense of 'be concerned about, care for, give aid'; the context is about caring.[36] However, this makes the last three members indistinct and the conclusion of Paul's list rather bland: the one who shares, the one who cares, the one who gives alms. While rhetoric may be wont to repetition, the point of Paul's body analogy here as in 1 Corinthians 12 must be the variety of the Spirit's inspiration, the difference of function of each member of the body, so we should not expect Romans 12: 8 effectively to conclude with a list of synonyms.

The sense of householder, host, and meeting-leader for *ho proïstamenos* in Rom. 12: 8 allows a more textured interpretation, and in fact reveals that Paul has in mind a particular sequence of events in the Christian gathering. The context of caring for the poor was within the early Christians' meal-fellowship. This actually distinguished the Christian process of almsgiving from that later claimed in Rabbinic sources for the synagogue, where money for food was taken to the local poor on the eve of the sabbath.[37] The Christians did things differently; they cared for their poor in the context of a meal within the private houses used for their meetings. This process probably had its roots in Jesus' meal-fellowship 'with tax-collectors and sinners' (Lk. 7: 30–32; 19: 7), and may be observed early in Acts, where (daily) distribution (Acts 6: 1) to any needy (2: 45; 4: 35) was made in the context of (daily) meals in private houses (Acts 2: 46). The meeting probably began with the spoken word and proceeded through an act of material sharing to a meal (the product of the sharing pocess) in the context of which bread was sacramentally broken, and finally prayer, the sequence given at Acts 2: 42: teaching, sharing (*koinōnia*), breaking of bread, the prayers.

We are dealing with a similar sequence at the end of Romans 12: 8 — those who hand gifts into the charge of the administrator at the meeting (those who 'contribute'), the leader himself (*proïstamenos*), who guides the collection of monies and the meal, and those who administer the distribution of alms (those who do 'acts of mercy'). The first element of the sequence, *ho metadidous*, indicates any members of the congregation who give material support. The sense of financial contribution can be clearly seen by comparing Ephesians 4: 28: 'Let the thief no longer steal, but rather let him labour, doing honest work with his hands, so that he may be able to give (RSV: *metadidonai*) to those in need.' Those who do 'acts of mercy' anticipate the 'deacons' of the later church, although they are not so called; they ensure the needy in the meeting are looked after, and then depart to look after those not able to attend the meeting; this care included the elements of the meal. The intervening *proïstamenos* is the host of each household group and overseer of the process of meal-fellowship and caring for the poor which took place under his auspices.

The plurality of *episkopoi* leading the Christians in the city of Philippi (Phil. 1: 1) are the same class of householders. The general context which we have discovered of prominent householders who maintain sub-groups of Christians in Corinth and Rome makes apparent that this text should not be regarded as somehow erratic or difficult to lay any store upon for understanding the church order of early Christianity. Clement probably understood it as referring to prominent householders, and therefore drew it into connection with 1 Cor. 16: 15. However, we should not assume that this leading class saw themselves as a ruling *council* or met as such. This idea arises partly through the assumption that the early Christians imitated the synagogue eldership, which as we have seen is unlikely. The assumption that the group of leaders at Philippi and in other churches of the Pauline mission constituted something like a *board of elders* is actually at the root of the problem of understanding the rise of the Ignatian order. They did not constitute a board or council in earlier times, but served their congregations as individual leaders, in this respect like later monarchical bishops. They only became a 'board' when the individual house congregations

permanently merged. As this happened, Christianity had to
recreate the single meal-president which the Christian liturgy had always demanded, creating a superior kind of overseer or bishop who was deemed to take the place of the
apostle both in terms of authority over the larger congregation and in terms of the taught tradition.

Servants at the Meal

In Greek the deacon or *diakonos* is a servant, often someone
who serves at table. The seven officers appointed in Acts 6:
1–6 as the solution to a problem over caring for widows in
the earliest congregation in Jerusalem have traditionally
been understood as the first appointed to the office of deacon
in the Christian church. The association is natural in view of
the rôle of the deacons in the later church in the practical
service of collection and distribution of alms. However, the
Seven appear to have been leaders of far greater status. The
term *diakonos* does not appear in the narrative, although the
cognate verb *diakonein* is used to describe the service at table
which the Twelve decline to take upon themselves (6: 2).
The appointment of the Seven is designed to solve the
problem of practical care for widows belonging to the group
of 'Hellenists' who appear in Acts 6: 1 as a group distinguish-
able from the 'Hebrews'; the latter are presumably the
disciple group gathered around the Twelve amongst whom a
poor-care system was operative (2: 42–47, 4: 32–5: 11).

Since all those appointed have Greek names, they seem
not to have been officers for the care of the poor in the whole
Christian community in Jerusalem, but only the 'Hellenist'
group. The distinction between 'Hellenists' and 'Hebrews'
in Acts 6: 1 seems to have been principally linguistic. All
living in Palestine in this period will have known some Greek.
The 'Hellenist' Christians appear not to have known Aramaic
and therefore not to have become integrated into the first
community of Jesus' disciples who worshipped in Aramaic.[38]
Rather, they remained in the context of synagogue congregations with strong links with the diaspora. These synagogues

are mentioned for the first time in Acts at this point (6: 9). Two of those mentioned in the account of the appointment of the Seven reappear in the rôles of preaching and teaching. Stephen teaches with disturbing effects in the Greek-speaking synagogues (6: 8–8: 1). Philip evangelises in Samaria (8: 4–13) Their rôle seems therefore to have been a combination of practical oversight of the poor-care system with teaching, evangelism, and overall leadership of the community of Greek-speaking Christians.

The distress of the Hellenist widows probably occurred because the Hellenist communities were growing at some social distance from the earliest community in the context of these synagogue congregations which worshipped in Greek. The solution to the widows' plight was to begin the formal organisation of the Christian community in this new social context by electing a formal leadership for them. The Seven represent at this stage something like the plurality of 'elder-bishops' which we have observed in the later Pauline congregations. They probably instituted meal-fellowship in their homes and each attended to the needs of a section of the group of Hellenist widows.

A more natural, though usually overlooked, point of the Acts story in which to see the early roots of the office of deacon is the daily table-fellowship which characterised the life of the Christian community in Jerusalem from earliest times (Acts 2: 46). The Hellenist widows had been excluded from a 'daily distribution' (Acts 6: 1) which clearly occurred in the context of this meal-fellowship, since the apostles declined to serve at tables to ensure fair shares for all. We have noted above that Acts 2: 42 probably gives the successive elements of the evening Christian meeting: 'the teaching of the apostles, the fellowship (*koinōnia*), the breaking of bread, and the prayers'. *Koinōnia* here indicates the process of collection of material contributions from those gathered for the evening meal and distribution of whatever was necessary to meet the needs of all.[39] This process of collection and distribution is also mentioned in Acts 2: 44–45. Clearly, before the dispute of Acts 6: 1 there was already a well-established daily round at the evening meal of collection and distribution to meet material needs. The references to possessions being laid at the apostles' feet (4: 35, 37; 5: 2) indicates that the apostles had overall charge of the community's financial and charitable arrangements. However, we should not assume from this that they took charge of all the practical tasks which the administration of such a system demanded. This is even more the case since the communitarian lifestyle which the earliest disciple-group in Jerusalem adopted was part of what we might term a wider communitarian stream in Judaism in this period. Amongst the Essenes there were formally organised property-sharing communities,[40] which bear some comparison with the first church in Jerusalem. The Pharisaic *chabûrah* (meal-fellowship) likewise expressed socially common religious feeling.

It is likely that service in the practicalities of the meal and the distribution of material goods devolved naturally on trustworthy younger men in the community, on the model of an office which already existed in such Jewish communities for such services. While natural honour was given to age in the ancient world, it was assumed that practical tasks of practical service would devolve naturally on the younger men of a community. Amongst the *Therapeutae* of Egypt, a Jewish ascetic sect which existed contemporaneously with the Acts events, young men serve at ritual meals and are called *diakonoi*.[41] The story of Ananias and Sapphira's deception of the Church in a matter of property in Acts 5: 1–11 gives a hint of the development of such an office of practical helper and servant. After the couple's fateful demise through Peter's powerful condemnation, both are taken out and buried as a matter of course by the 'young men' of the community (5: 6, *neōteroi*; 10, *neaniskoi*).

Since meal-fellowship occurred in the context of private homes in the early Jerusalem church, the householders of those homes will have presided at the meals. This may be an important clue for understanding the increasingly prominent 'elders' of the Jerusalem church (Acts 11: 30; 15: 2, 6, 23; 21: 18), a group whose enigmatic appearance in the narrative of

Acts has proved problematic for commentators. As we have seen, in the Pauline communities the householder would command the proceedings of the meeting within his house and preside at the meal, and be assisted by his household servants (who had probably all adopted the new faith) or others of the congregation in the administration of it. Pliny the younger tortured 'two maidservants who were called deaconesses' to learn about the Christian 'superstition'.[42] The two women were probably slaves who took on the rôle of service at the meal in their own household or in another where they attended Christian worship. Where we learn of the conversion of whole households in Acts, we hear mention of the trusted servants of the houses. When the God-fearing Cornelius has his vision, he sends two of his servants 'and a devout (God-fearing) soldier from among those who waited on him' (10: 7) to fetch Peter to explain the vision. Peter finds the whole house ready to listen (10: 27) who all believe and submit to baptism (10: 44–48) so that the whole 'household' is saved (11: 14). Such trusted servants will have served at the first meal-fellowship, and may have been later joined by other believers from the congregation who became 'honorary' servants within the household for the occasion of the meal. Here we have the generation of the local ministry of *episkopoi* and *diakonoi*. *Diakonoi* were those who served at meals for the householder; hence there was always a plurality in later Christianity, whose connection with the *episkopos* was intimate. The *episkopos* was a leading Christian householder in the city who with the apostles' approval had sponsored the Christian message by giving over his house to the church for meetings and the Christian meal, which he organised and at which he presided. He was the 'overseer' of the section of the Christian congregation which met in his house. These were the people Paul referred to in Thessalonica as 'those who labour among you and are over you as patrons in the Lord and admonish you' (1 Thess. 5: 12).

These householders probably came to have a rôle in the collection and oversight of church funds. In 1 Cor. 16: 1–3 Paul instructs the Corinthians: 'Now concerning the collection

for the saints . . . On the first day of the week, let each of you
put something aside, putting in store as he may prosper, that
no collections be made when I come.' The text does not
make sense if the 'putting in store' phrase is taken to refer
to a private, personal accumulation of the individual believer's donations before Paul's arrival. The 'first day of the
week' was the day on which Christians assembled, and must
be mentioned because the collection takes place publicly on
that weekly occasion. Furthermore, these weekly collections
alleviate the necessity for collections after arrival; they mean
the church will have the money to hand already collected.[43]
Since the only premises which the Christians had were those
of the better-off householders, these funds will have been
stored under the oversight of these householders. There may
be a hint of the financial offices of these householders in
Paul's specific address to the 'bishops and deacons' at
Philippi (Phil 1: 1), since his letter concludes with carefully
composed thanks for material support (4: 10–20), and the
matter of finance may determine much of the earlier argument of the letter.[44] The officers with these functions are
probably the *antilēmpseis* and *kybernēseis* of 1 Cor. 12.28. The
Revised Standard Version translates the former group as
'helpers', since *antilambanein* may mean 'take someone's part,
help, come to the aid of'.[45] In the conclusion of Paul's speech
to the Ephesian elders, where he comments on finances in
the church (Acts 20: 33–36) the verb refers to the assistance
of the weak or sick with financial resources (v. 35). The
'helpers' of 1 Cor. 12: 28, then, show the nascent diaconate,
while the 'administrators' who follow are the householder
meal-presidents.

The Emergence of the Monarchical Episcopate

In later Christianity, the rôle of presiding at the eucharist was
restricted to bishops and elders. This suggests that the
elders had always presided at the Christian meal, and coheres
with the social origins which we have suggested for this group
as the prominent householders who hosted the early house-

groups and led their meal-fellowship. By the time of Ignatius, the 'elders' are no longer heads of smaller house-church meal-fellowship groups, but assemble as a council grouped around the monarchical bishop. As we have seen, the regular worship situation which Ignatius describes is therefore far too large to occur in the protected space of the atrium of a single house, however grand. By Ignatius' time, gathering places of a more substantial scale for Christians must have been created. The most natural way to achieve spaces of these physical dimensions would be to modify private homes which had passed into the possession of the community by replacing internal walls with arches supporting the roof and building into the courtyard space. The early Christian church discovered at Capernaum was based originally on a room in a private house and gives evidence of such extension.[46] The church at Dura-Europos was based on a private house, but with the atrium space modified by the removal of an internal dividing wall.[47]

The creation of larger meeting spaces would enable the regular gathering of the household congregations of a city together in one place, and Ignatius' description implies that this became the normal practice. As we have seen above, the combining of individual house-groups into a larger congregation explains the awkwardness of what Ignatius saw as symbolised by each office of the threefold order. In this development, the heads of individual household congregations, who had been used to presiding alone at the eucharists in their homes, coalesced into an assembled body carrying some authority, prominent in the proceedings of the larger, united meeting. At this point in the church's social development we see the emergence of a council of elders, prominent in the meeting. Previously, this group would only have appeared at larger gatherings when the house-churches exceptionally came together. They were not in earlier times a council in the sense that they would meet together independently of their household congregations or could co-opt to their 'membership' any of the congregation. They were merely the group of trusted householders in whose homes

Christian worship was normally conducted. The development of the elder-council visible with Ignatius probably happened alongside the detachment of the taking of the eucharistic elements from the context of a full fellowship meal, since full meals could only be taken in the household context, which became less significant or was even discouraged as a place for Christians to meet.

As we have noted, this transition in the social development of the Church shows that the appearance of a council of elders in the church of a city was not simply an imitation of Jewish synagogue practice. The assembly of Christian elders may have appeared increasingly like the elders of the Jewish community, but key differences remained due to the difference of origins. While the synagogue elders had no rôle in the assembly's worship, the Christian elders had a rôle because they had previously functioned as elder-bishops who had the oversight of individual house-churches, presided at their eucharists, and had a rôle in teaching and discipline. The single elder-bishops of the earlier, individual house-church congregations will have been used to assembling in this fashion on the occasions when the assembly of all believers in the city was required. In terms of physical arrangements, whereas the senior members of the synagogue community probably had preeminence in the seating order as part of the worshipping congregation, the Christian elders were seated facing the congregation, as Ignatius implies, with the bishop, since they had previously presided at the household-eucharists.

Lightfoot's famous explanation for the rise of the monarchical episcopate was that each church had been led by a board of elder-bishops. Since a board must have a chair, the elder-bishop who chaired the board of elders will have had a powerful position. An elder-bishop who gained the chairmanship permanently will have come permanently to possess a position superior to the other elder-bishops, and will have become *the* bishop, the monarchical bishop of Ignatius.[48] The position outlined can support a revision of Lightfoot's view. As the elder-bishops of individual congregations became a regularly assembled group leading the larger type of congregation, in some congregations the most senior or most respected may have come regularly to preside at the eucharist of the larger meeting. An elder-bishop who came to receive the honour of presiding at the larger meeting permanently would become the head of the whole Christian community in the city, for he would gain a principal rôle in matters of discipline (exclusion from the Lord's table), and would probably assume responsibility for the upkeep of the building and thereby gain ultimate control of the church's meeting place.

Such may have happened. But the development cannot be assumed without certain qualifications. First, the earlier elder-bishop class did not possess the peripatetics' right of support from the community, and in social terms did not need it. They were community worthies whose position had arisen partly out of their social status and wealth. They had thus been used to protecting congregations as patrons, rather than being in their pay as officers. They may, therefore, have taken the leadership in larger meetings, but in doing this they will have been conscious that they thereby assumed a social rôle different from that of leading a household congregation. They were of the wealthier social class who had businesses or estates to run; if they took on the leadership rôle of larger congregations, they may have had to give up other responsibilities and enter full-time service for the church. This renunciation of a worldly for a spiritual calling previously defined the peripatetics in social terms. They largely crossed, therefore, the social boundary which previously existed between them and the peripatetic class. The elder at 1 Tim. 5: 17 who serves (*proestōtes*, presides) well sounds like one who was crossing over to a different kind of Christian service, and beginning to receive the remuneration which had previously been the preserve of the peripatetic class.

Second, elder-bishops were used to thinking of themselves as the second rank in the church's authority pattern. They had gained and retained their authority through the approval of the visiting apostles, and we cannot assume that they would readily have taken on an authority-rôle above the level of the house-congregation which they had served at the apostles' behest. A picture from their previous experience illustrates this. The house-churches will have been most used to gathering *en masse* in one place (as we have noted, probably the courtyard of a larger house) for particular important occasions in the community's life. The commonest occasions for such specially arranged larger gatherings in the early decades of the church's life will often have been the visit of an apostle, prophet, or revered teacher to the city. If the elder-bishop presided on such occasions, he did so as the host, but aware that the visitor was the greater and principal authority. Those gathered came to hear the visitor, not the householder. Indeed, the householder elder-bishops may always have understood that they held a pre-eminent rôle only in the absence of the peripatetics whose activities had founded their own congregations.

Third, the coming to pre-eminence of a single, local elder-bishop in larger meetings could not have happened without the express approval of other elder-bishops, who had been used to exercising authority over the house-church groups which merged into the larger assembly. The dignity of each constitutive house-church would have been impugned if the grounds on which a single elder-bishop should gain preeminence over all the previously independent household groups were not clearly articulated.[49] All these factors suggest that if a local elder-bishop came to have preeminence in the larger meeting, he would have been well aware of a transition to a different order within the authority-pattern of the church, and that this would have been acknowledged through a formal ordination to office which indicated the approval of the congregation.

The *Didachē* gives us another picture of the process of creation of other monarchical bishops in this period. We learn of the settlement of worthy peripatetics in local communities, who clearly come to have a pre-eminent rôle as monarchical leaders of the communities. The *Didachē* implies that such settling peripatetics would retain their right of support from the community. It has frequently been maintained that Timothy and Titus represent an increasingly localised class of 'apostolic delegates' who were the precursors of the permanently local monarchical bishop.[50] It is worth noting that as individual peripatetics simply grew older there would be a natural tendency for them to settle in one location for longer periods, and eventually permanently.[51] It is not difficult to imagine that both processes, the elevation of local, much-respected elders, and the settlement of worthy peripatetics, contributed to the creation of monarchical bishops of equal status. The monarchical bishops who emerged to head the larger, combined congregations were local officers on a grander scale, which transcended that of the earlier house-churches, and were in effect the replacement for the peripatetic class. Some of them were probably aging peripatetics who settled in one city of their earlier mission fields, and thereby automatically enjoyed authority above the level of the elder-bishops and retained their right to support from the community. Others were probably raised by deliberate act from the rank of elder-bishop to overseer of all the Christians in the city, and received payment because their responsibilities were thereby greatly expanded.[52]

Thus questions of social context help explain the rise of the threefold pattern of offices in the church. It has become apparent that the threefold order was present in the churches of the early decades in the pattern of a peripatetic class, a local householder / elder-bishop class, and the class of servants at the Christian meal. This order became the pattern of the monarchical bishop of the city, his council of elders, and the deacons who served the poor and at the eucharist. This transition involved not merely the creation of a local equivalent to the peripatetic class, but also the coalescing of the elder-bishop class into the council of elders with the creation of larger meeting spaces. This evolution speaks for the liveliness of the Christian community, which could adjust its structures to the changing situation. The principal changes have much to do with the very success of the earlier peripatetic class. As areas became evangelised, it became less meaningful to have a peripatetic class which simply rotated between mature congregations, but necessary to have local leaders of stature to govern what had become very large local communities and even to defend them against the doctrinal innovations which were abroad. The class of peripatetics gave way to the class of monarchical bishops to secure what the peripatetics had first created.

The Ministry of the Laity and the Social Scale of the Congregation

The downside of the creation and securing of larger congregations was a stifling of the laity's rôle. Between Paul and Ignatius we find the presentation of Ephesians, in the latter part of the first century, probably written by a disciple of Paul *c.* AD 80–90. The beginnings of the creation of the monarchical episcopate are probably detectable in the conclusion of the list of Christ's gifts to the Church at 4: 11–12:

> And his gifts were that some should be apostles, some prophets, some evangelists, some teacher-shepherds, to equip the saints, for the work of ministry, for building up the body of Christ.

Here the presentation of Paul's triad of 'apostles', 'prophets' and 'teachers' (1 Cor. 12: 28) undergoes modification. The author ranks a class of probably peripatetic preachers after the apostles and prophets, denoting them 'evangelists'. They are neither prophets nor apostles, since for the author these groups were historical and could not be augmented. Hence at 2: 20 the author speaks of the 'foundation of the apostles and prophets', as of a group fading into history; the author apparently does not wish to use of current peripatetics the terms 'apostles' and 'prophets' as did the author of the *Didachē*. With the desire to see doctrinal uniformity based on the teaching of the earlier peripatetic class, the status of current peripatetics receives qualification. Following the classification of the remaining acceptable peripatetics as 'evangelists', Paul's triad is further modified by calling the teachers something like 'shepherd-teachers'. The Greek has an article before every element of this list until it concludes with 'the shepherds and teachers'; hence these two words denote one group, shepherd-teachers. Teachers have become shepherd-teachers because they are now settled in one location, permanently maintained by a local church, rather than being mobile as previously. The term 'shepherd' is added to denote the localised nature of their service.

The translation given above of Ephesians 4: 11–12 places a comma after the phrase 'to equip the saints' thus making the subsequent phrase merely its repetition in other words, 'to equip the saints, for the work of ministry'. Without the comma, the text predicates 'ministry' of all 'the saints'. The presence or absence of the comma is a decision for the translator. Given above is the punctuation of the King James Version, the Revised Version, and the first edition of the Revised Standard Version, which all include the comma. Since the edition of the Revised Standard Version known as the Common Bible, the comma has been omitted, hence predicating 'ministry' of 'the saints'. Did the author of Ephesians undertand that all the saints, all believers, had a contribution of 'ministry' (translations without the comma), or had he come to see 'ministry' as the preserve of those principal officers of the church which he lists? If the author were the original Paul, it would be clear that no comma should be present. However, the author is probably not the original Paul, and the translation with the comma probably does give his sense. The key point in favour of the presence of the comma, and the telling denial of 'ministry' to all believers, is the shortness of the list of gifts. In 1 Cor. 12: 8–11 Paul gave nine examples of the Spirit's working, in 1 Cor. 12: 28 his list has eight elements, and in Romans 12: 3–8 seven. All contain elements which are, in our terms, transparently 'lay' ministries — the vocal gifts through which the Spirit's wisdom enters the congregation through all its members, and even the simple task of giving material contributions at the eucharist for the sake of the poor. The author of Ephesians, however, has effectively drawn off the three principal offices which open 1 Cor. 12: 28, modified

them to his own church situation, in which the maintenance
of doctrinal continuity with the apostolic tradition has become paramount, and stopped there. 'Ministry' (*diakonia*) has
thus become the preserve only of the leading classes of
officers over the congregation. The gifts which would be
called 'lay' ministry in our parlance are simply omitted. So,
losing the original apostolic vision of Paul, ministry has become the preserve of certain of the church's officers; both
the laity and the nascent diaconate are excluded.[53]

The process of the exclusion of the laity from ministry,
then, is even detectable in one of the later New Testament
writings. However, that the original vision of Paul faded in
the mind of the Church was due, if the thesis offered in this
paper on the rise of the threefold ministry is correct, not to
a usurpation of the laity by the emerging clergy, but to the
scale of the gathered city congregations which emerged
because of the success of the mission and the need to exclude
heterodox teaching. Congregations of hundreds of souls *could
not* use the gifts of lay individuals as could the early house-
churches of two or three dozen. The later and yet more
immense success of the gospel resulted, by a further change,
in what is largely the present structure of the Catholic
churches, with so many congregations that only one ordained
elder (priest) was allotted to each. However, the witness of
Paul has been preserved for us, and the Church may, like the
scribe trained for the Kingdom, bring both old and new from
its household treasury (Matt. 13: 52). Paul's emphasis on the
public working of the Spirit through each member of the
congregation is grounded in the understanding of the Church
attested elsewhere in the New Testament. The Church,
representing the age of fulfilment, in which all the members
of God's renewed people are possessed by the Spirit, is
contrasted with the time of expectation, in which the Spirit
worked only through the inspired few. As Peter expounded
on the day of Pentecost, in the last days the Spirit is out-
poured upon the whole congregation (Acts 2: 15–21, quoting
Joel 2: 28–32). Paul understands this theological existence
of the Church, as the community in which all minister

through the Spirit, as socially realised in the local congregation to which all make contribution through the Spirit. The contemporary Church must always be prepared to allow the development outlined in this paper to be reversed. Larger congregations can only encourage lay ministry through the creation of a cellular structure which encourages, guides and nurtures the development of individual lay gifts. Where congregations are small, the Church is right to look to its earliest social forms and allow certain tasks in public worship to be met through the gifts invested in the laity to sustain the local Body of Christ. Perhaps there is even a rôle, where no church building can be maintained, for the re-employment of the house-church pattern.

Notes

1. W. Telfer, *The Office of a Bishop* (London, Darton, Longman and Todd, 1962), p. 69.
2. W. Meeks, *The First Urban Christians* (New Haven, Yale UP, 1983), p. 75.
3. cf. A. Maiuri, *Ercolano*, I (Rome, 1958) 198, 208, 266, 280, 384, 394; A. G. McKay, *Houses, Villas, and Palaces in the Roman World* (London, 1975); H. Eschebach, *Pompeii* (Leipzig, 1978) 312; E. E. Ellis, *Pauline Theology: Ministry and Society* (Exeter, Paternoster, 1989), pp. 140–141.
4. The meal could be taken in the adjacent dining room, which was normally smaller, however.
5. Ignatius, *Magnesians* 6; *Trallians* 3.
6. Ignatius, *Magnesians* 6; *Trallians* 3.
7. cf. E. Käsemann, 'Ministry and Community in the New Testament', in his *Essays on New Testament Themes* (London, SCM, 1964), pp. 63–94.
8. R. Sohm, *Kirchenrecht I. Die Geschichtlichen Grundlagen* (Leipzig, 1892) pp. 158–164. Sohm thought the Church mistakenly transformed charism into permanent office. The lively debate which has ensued is surveyed in E. Nardoni, 'Charism in the Early Church since Rudolph Sohm: An Ecumenical Challenge', *Theological Studies* 53 (1992), pp. 646–662.
9. The 'South Galatian' theory would place Galatians earlier.
10. J. T. Burtchaell, *From Synagogue to Church* (Cambridge, CUP, 1992).

11. cf. H.W. Beyer, art. *diakonos*, in the *Theological Dictionary of the New Testament* (hereafter TDNT) Vol. II, ed. G. Kittel et al., translated G.W. Bromiley (Grand Rapids, Eerdmans, 1964), pp. 88–93, see p. 91.

12. The terminological and other evidence against the synagogue derivation of Christian 'elders' is surveyed by A. E. Harvey, 'Elders', *Journal of Theological Studies* n.s. 25 (1974), pp. 318–332. R. A. Campbell, 'The Elders of the Jerusalem Church', *Journal of Theological Studies* n.s. 44 (1993), pp. 511–528, comes to the same rejection of the proposed synagogue model for Christian elders, see especially p. 513. cf. also F. Young, *The Theology of the Pastoral Letters* (Cambridge, CUP, 1994), pp. 109–110.

13. A.E. Harvey comes to the same judgement in his review of Burtchaell in *Journal of Theological Studies* n.s. 44 (1993) pp. 678–679.

14. A von Harnack, *The Expansion of Christianity in the First Three Centuries* (London, Williams & Norgate, 1904); *The Mission and Expansion of Christianity in the First Three Centuries* (New York, Harper, 1961) Vol. I, pp. 319–368; *The Constitution & Law of the Church in the First Two Centuries* (London, Williams & Norgate, 1910), pp. 23–25.

15. The other criticisms of Harnack, in J. A. Robinson, 'The Christian Ministry in the Apostolic and sub-Apostolic periods', in *Essays on the Early History of the Church and the Ministry*, ed. H. B. Swete (London, Macmillan, 1921), pp. 57–92, are less persuasive.

16. This, although disputed, is probably the meaning of the text. The texts subsequently cited at 1 Tim. 5: 18 (Deut. 25: 4 and 24: 15) had earlier close connections with the support of the apostles (cf. 1 Cor. 9: 9, 14; Lev. 19: 13; Matt. 10: 10; Lk. 10: 7). The word usually translated 'honour' could indicate 'honorarium'. cf. F. Young, op. cit., pp. 105–106.

17. cf. Bengst Holmberg, *Paul and Power* (Lund, CWK Gleerup, 1978), p. 97.

18. cf. J. D. G. Dunn, *Jesus and the Spirit* (London, SCM, 1975), p. 280.

19. The apostle who wishes to stay for three days is a false prophet (XI.4–5). The prophet who eats food ordered in a trance or demands money in a trance is a false prophet (XI.9, 12).

20. Esp. E. Hatch, *The Organisation of the Early Christian Churches* (London, 1881).

21. Although there are instances of clubs meeting in households, Wayne Meeks is generally negative about the possible rele-

vance of the clubs for the social form of the Christian churches, *The First Urban Christians* (New Haven, Yale UP, 1983), pp. 77–80.

22. E. E. Ellis, op. cit., p. 141, thinks that the earliest reference to church buildings is Clement of Alexandria, *Stromata* 7.5 (*c.* AD 200). It is probable that prior to this private houses had been extended with special meeting facilities, or were modified for use in their entirety as church buildings as they passed into the possession of the Christian communities.

23. cf. 1 Cor. 1: 14; comparison with the mention of baptising the household of Stephanas in the following verse shows that their names here stand for the baptism of their whole households.

24. cf. also 1 Clement 44.

25. cf. C. K. Barrett, *Church, Ministry and Sacraments in the New Testament* (Carlisle, Paternoster, 1985) p. 36.

26. G. Theissen, *The Social Setting of Pauline Christianity* (Edinburgh, T. & T. Clark, 1982), pp. 73–96.

27. op. cit., 107. C. K. Barrett, op.cit., p. 37, comments more pragmatically: 'a few . . . who have money, education, influence; who are accustomed to leadership . . . who have large and pleasant houses . . . especially if they came into the church in its early days and have, through long acquaintance with Paul, a good grasp of Christian belief and practice, will gravitate into positions of leadership . . . It is common sense . . . it is social inevitability.' Perhaps this does not allow Paul's intention sufficient scope.

28. cf. B. Reicke TDNT VI, 700–701; W. Bauer, W.F. Arndt, and F.W. Gingrich, *A Greek-English Lexicon of the New Testament and Other Early Christian Literature* (Chicago, University of Chicago Press, 1979: hereafter Bauer-Arndt-Gingrich), p. 707.

29. e.g. both Josephus (*Vita* 168) and 1 Maccabees 5: 19 use the verb of the government of the congregation (here *plethos*, which is a technical term designating the community which gathers in council to make decisions), cf. Bauer-Arndt-Gingrich p. 668 and compare the use of the Hebrew *rab* in the Rule of the Community from Qumran (1QS) V: 2, 9, 22; VI: 19.

30. E. Best, *A Commentary on the First and Second Epistles to the Thessalonians* (London, Black, 1977), pp. 223–224.

31. cf. ad loc. E. von Dobschütz, *Die Thessalonischer-Briefe* (Göttingen, 1909); M. Dibelius, *An die Thessalonischer I, II: An die Philipper* (Tübingen, 1937); E. Best, op. cit.; cf. W. Meeks, op.cit., pp. 134, 234.

32. Bauer-Arndt-Gingrich p. 718.

33. op.cit., p. 134.

34. Especially as *patria potestas* in the Roman context.
35. cf. E. E. Ellis, op.cit., p. 37.
36. cf. J. D. G. Dunn, *Romans 9–16* (Dallas Texas, Word Books, 1988) p. 731; B. Reicke, TDNT VI, 701.
37. The transient poor were given food on a daily basis from the 'tray', but were not invited into people's houses for meals. cf. G. F. Moore, *Judaism* (Cambridge Mass., 1927), pp. 174–178. Moore does not assume this system operated in the synagogue in the first century, and commentators who assume that it did and may therefore have provided a model for Christian activity are opposed by D. Seccombe, 'Was there organised charity in Jerusalem before the Christians?' *Journal of Theological Studies* n. s. 29(1978), pp. 140–143.
38. cf. M. Hengel, *Between Jesus and Paul* (London, SCM, 1983), pp. 1–29, 133–156.
39. We may assume principally clothing such as the widow Tabitha was used to manufacture at Joppa, Acts 9: 32–43. The character of the 'daily distribution' may bear comparison with the daily process of meal-fellowship in the Essene camps described in Philo, *Hypothetica*, 11: 8–13. Here, individual members labour outside the community and bring home their wages to be consigned to the common funds at the end of the working day. Then the camp overseer takes the money and purchases all that the community needs, including food for the evening meal, at which a process of distribution must take place. In the context of the description there is particular emphasis on provision for the old and sick, who could make no contribution but have the right to participate in the common meal, as in Acts 6: 1.
40. cf. B. J. Capper 'The Interpretation of Acts 5: 4', *Journal for the Study of the New Testament* 19 (1983), pp. 117–131 and R. Riesner, 'Essener und Urkirche in Jerusalem' *Bibel und Kirche* 40 (1985), pp. 64–76.
41. Philo, *On the Contemplative Life*, 70–71.
42. Pliny, *Epistles*, X: 96.
43. For further argumentation for this view cf. E. E. Ellis, op.cit., pp. 94–95.
44. cf. B. J. Capper, 'Paul's Dispute with Philippi: Understanding Paul's Argument in Phil. 1–2 from his Thanks in 4: 10–20', *Theologische Zeitschrift* 49 (1993), pp. 193–214.
45. Bauer-Arndt-Gingrich, 74.
46. cf. E. M. Meyers and James F. Strange, *Archaeology, the Rabbis, and Early Christianity* (London, SCM, 1981), pp. 58–61, 128–130.

47. C. H. Kraeling, *The Christian Building* (*Excavations at Dura-Europos, Final Report*, VIII, Part II, ed. M. I. Rostotzeff et al., London, OUP, 1943ff), pp. 7–30.

48. J. B. Lightfoot, Excursus 'The Christian Ministry' in *The Epistles of St. Paul. Philippians* (London, Macmillan, 1888), pp. 181–269.

49. This is probably the issue about Diotrephes in 3 John.

50. This is argued by B. S. Easton, *The Pastoral Epistles* (London, SCM, 1948) pp. 171–179. In the subscriptions of the manuscript tradition Titus is called Bishop of the Cretans, Timothy Bishop of the Ephesians, cf. Bauer-Arndt-Gingrich, 299.

51. This may have been a very important factor in the process which generated the class of monarchical bishops.

52. It is possible that the group of elder-bishops sought younger men with energies suited to the task to lead the joined city congregations. A view of this type, which makes the monarchical bishop effectively the appointee of the elders, is put forward by F. M. Young, 'On *Episkopos* and *Presbyteros*', *Journal of Theological Studies* n.s. 45 (1994), pp. 142–148. This development is, however, less likely in view of the sheer authority claimed for the later monarchical bishop, who must have been a figure of some stature to preside above the elders at the community gathering.

53. The issue of the comma is much disputed. For a judicious treatment of the passage which supports the understanding given here, see A. M. Lincoln, *Ephesians* (Dallas, Word, 1990), pp. 253–254.

4

The Laity in the Ministry
of the Church

John Halliburton

> To the high priest special duties are allotted, the priests have
> their own place, the levites are occupied in service and the
> laity do what is required of the laity.[1]

Clement, Bishop of Rome at the end of the first century,
wrote this to a Greek church the story of whose troubles had
reached him across the Aegean sea. Why Clement in Rome
should be worried about Corinth in Greece is not at first
immediately clear — a legacy perhaps from the Apostle Paul
who had already washed a good deal of Corinthian dirty linen
in public. Apparently, as in St Paul's day, there were still
factions at Corinth and one party in the church had risen up
against the presbyters and deposed them. Clement, being
appealed to, wrote a letter of some length, the greater part
of it being an exhortation to repentance and peace, and the
tail giving some practical guidance. The church cannot prosper, writes Clement, unless its divinely given order is respected. As under the old Covenant, the high priest had
special duties, the priest knew his place, the levite was
engaged in service of the sanctuary and the laypeople did
what was appropriate for laity to do; so under the new
covenant each person in his or her own order must take part

in the liturgy and life of the church. Clement here sees what he believes the Old Testament hierarchy to be as a shadow or type of the Christian structure of ministry. He himself does not spell out exactly how this typology is to be understood; but contemporary and later Christian literature[2] will lose no time in identifying the bishop as the high priest, the presbyter as the priest, the deacon as the levite and the laity as the laity. So it is to be for generations to come; and the laity look like being for ever the bottom of the pile.

Clement is here using the adjective *laikos* to mean 'layman' and the word is often used in the plural to mean collectively 'the laity'. Though in this form it regularly refers to laity in the narrower sense of a group or *tagma* in the church as distinct from the clergy,[3] it has to be borne in mind that ultimately *laikos* derives from the Greek *laos*, which in turn translates the Hebrew *am*. In Old Testament times, 'people' was not simply a collective term for a crowd of human beings, but signified a particular people who belonged to a particular land — race, tribe almost.[4] The *am ha arets* were the people who lawfully occupied a territory — the Egyptians in Egypt, the Canaanites in Canaan for example. Those who wandered through the territories of others were 'not a people', and until settled, the Israelites were in just such a state, both in Egypt and on their journey before the settlement. But once arrived in the land which they believed totally given over to them, they were supremely God's people. Hence the threat in Hosea of being called *Lo ammi* i.e. 'not a people' was a dire one,[5] and meant losing the land as well as their identity and being scattered throughout the other nations. But Hosea also has a word of hope.[6] 'I will sow her unto me in the earth (*arets*)', he says, 'And I will have mercy upon her that had not obtained mercy; and I will say to them which were not my people, Thou art my people; and they shall say, Thou art my God.'

It is undoubtedly to this understanding of 'the people' that the author of 1 Peter is referring, addressing scattered congregations in Asia Minor, many of them probably pagan converts. The letter shows quite plainly that the inheritance of God's promise to his own people has now passed very clearly to the Christian community.[7] It is those who are now gathered around the new cornerstone in Zion who are the elect of God, a 'holy nation', a 'people for God's own possession'. It is they who, as living stones, make up the new temple of God for the offering of spiritual sacrifices. It is they who collectively constitute the royal priesthood (*hierateuma*) for the offering of these sacrifices (cf. Revelation 1: 6. 'And he made us to be a kingdom to be priests unto his God and Father'). All of this is very important for congregations miles from Jerusalem. They need on the one hand a sense of solidarity, of being a people who 'belong together' by their common calling, just as solidly as in the racial bonds of historic Judaism. And they need also to know that this is a new situation; they were once 'not a people';[8] but by virtue of their baptism into and faith in Christ, crucified and risen, they are now as much God's people and God's temple[9] as if they were actually domiciled in the Holy Land.

By this account, all the traditional hierarchy of the Old Testament structures would at first sight have seemed to have disappeared. The whole people is the priesthood, the whole people is the Temple, the whole people, according to several New Testament sources, offer spiritual sacrifices, offer themselves in service.[10] The whole cult in other words seems to have been lifted out of Jerusalem, spiritualised and re-established elsewhere. Why then the need for a Christian hierarchy if Christ alone is the true high priest and all the people of God are a kingdom and priests,[11] a royal priesthood and a holy nation?[12]

No human community of course can exist without structures, and without some pattern of authority. The new people of God from the earliest times believed that there was a givenness about the most essential structures. Local churches may have had elders and overseers, responsible members thrown up by the community to which the local church itself gave authority and recognition. But there is also another and very important strand in early church thinking which saw presbyters and bishops (in those days interchangeable terms) not merely selected by the community but given divine authority by the act of the laying-on of hands with prayer. Clement of Rome himself declares that Jesus Christ sent the apostles and the apostles commissioned others (i.e. the presbyter / bishops of the local churches). And by the end of the second century, no church could claim genuine apostolicity and catholicity unless it could equally prove that its presiding bishop stood in direct succession to the apostles themselves. Deacons from the earliest times were regularly ordained and appointed and seen as integral to the administration and pastoral care of any church community; and in course of time, as the church spread to the suburbs and thence to the countryside, the bishop had to appoint and ordain those whom he called presbyters to care for suburban and village churches and their congregations.[13]

The ordained ministry, however, grew up in the context of a community which understood each and every member to have an essential rôle to play. The doctrine of the Church as the Body of Christ was not invented by St Paul but derives most probably not from the Greek concept of the body corporate but from the Rabbinic notion of all mankind being incorporated into the body of Adam.[14] Scythians formed his forefinger, Libyans his big toe and so on until every limb and organ was complete. In the first-century Rabbinic understanding therefore, all nations belonged to God's purpose, all nations were part of God's plan for redemption and would one day come into that temple which God would reveal at the end of the age.[15] When St Paul in the fifth chapter of the Epistle to the Romans talks of mankind being transported from being 'in Adam' to being 'in Christ'[16] he takes hold of this vision and transforms it to see the whole of mankind being mystically incorporated into the Body of Christ, the Second Adam, into the new human race which Christ had united to himself. It follows that of this new redeemed humanity every local church is a kind of microcosm. In other words, the picture of the unity of mankind at the universal level is mirrored microcosmically in the cosmopolitan churches of mixed race and colour at the local level. They are mankind writ small, pictures of the potential unity and harmony of the human race.

Paul goes on to say that this picture is incomplete if anything goes wrong with any of its constituent parts. If one member rejoices, all the members rejoice. But if one suffers, then all suffer.[17] Each individual Christian is therefore integral in his or her ministry to the work of the whole. No one ministry is more important than another; and there are many ministries — apostles, prophets, governments, helps, gifts of healing, gifts of speaking in tongues, interpreting tongues.[18] Among these, the ordained ministry is only one, and, by its very nature, exists to serve the rest. For the pattern of ministry taught by Christ to the apostles[19] is not one of lording it over the laity, but rather a way of service to the rest of the church in order that its members may use their God-given gifts to the greatest advantage.

Why then the laity at the bottom of the pile? Why this adoption of the term *laikos* to signify almost 'the common people' as opposed to the whole noble race responding to the call of God? Some, writing about the laity in the early church, have accepted that the laity were the people in the pew and not in the sanctuary, and have concentrated simply on what the laity were allowed to do within the Christian community. Could they preach, could they baptise, could they teach? Or were all these functions strictly reserved to the clergy? Initiation of course was for a long time the task of the bishop alone, though it is admitted that a layperson could baptise in emergency. Preaching too was primarily the bishop's task, though a presbyter might substitute if the bishop were not present. But by the fourth century, the laity were being classed as a particular *tagma*, different from the clergy, different from the widows, virgins and ascetics. They had their own place in church; they should not usurp the place of the clergy in the sanctuary. They were not to preach, not to bless the *agapē*. At the eucharist, their sole contribution was to say 'Amen' at the giving of thanks. They might assist the bishop in advising about the reconciliation of penitents, might advise too about suitable candidates for the priesthood. But apart from that, they needed to know their place, come to church and do their job in the world.[20]

There were however certain responsibilities within the Christian community at which some laypeople excelled and established a considerable reputation, such as teaching. Two of the most famous schools in the ancient world, those of Justin Martyr at Rome and of Clement and Origen at Alexandria were founded and led by those very definitely not in holy orders, and in this they commanded considerable authority. When Origen left Egypt for Caesarea, he very properly resisted the challenge that he should not teach if he were not ordained and somewhat reluctantly accepted ordination as presbyter. But the catechetical schools on the Rome / Alexandria axis were a powerful influence in the ancient world and a testimony to the front-line influence of lay people.[21]

So also were the confessors, those who went to prison in time of persecution or were executed for confessing their faith. In the eyes of the church, the lay confessor in prison had far more credibility and authority than a presbyter. So in the years which followed the persecutions did the monk who went out into the desert. Early monasticism was a predominantly lay movement.[22] Years of solitude and austerity of living made of the followers of Antony and Pachomius men of great wisdom and discernment, compared to the feckless and feeble social entrepreneurs who had ingratiated themselves into the ranks of the clergy and whom Jerome ridicules from his eyrie in the deserts of Chalcis.[23] But when the ascetics returned to the world they found the world they had left astonished and wondering, listening and respecting, more eager to listen to the holy man than to hear the bishop. It is recorded by John Moschos, author of the *Sacred Praire*, that a certain monk had a dream about his monastic brother. He tells him that he had dreamed of him up to his waist in the Lake of Fire threatened in the Book of Revelation. His brother replied, 'Do you know why I was standing only up to my waist in the Lake of Fire?' 'No', said his accuser. 'Well, I will tell you', said his brother. 'I was standing on the shoul-

ders of the bishop.'[24] As in our own day, the media of the
ancient world, travelogue and hagiographer, made much
more of examples of outstanding holiness than they did of
the fortunes or failures of the institutional church. In literary
circles in Rome, Sulpicius Severus on St Martin and Palladius
on the monks of Egypt made much better reading than the
chroniclers of ecclesiastical controversy. And in the villages,
the local monk was often much more highly valued than the
local clergy. When Adam the Silent, for example, first came
to his village, barricaded himself into his cell and began to
sing psalms, the locals piled heaps of filthy refuse at his front
door. But when local government officials arrived to collect
the taxes, it was the monk who negotiated a deal and settled
the terms.[25] Holiness meant practical wisdom, as the eastern
churches realised when they sent messengers to the pillar
saint, Simeon Stylites to ask his advice about a political and
theological crisis in the church at the time of the Council of
Ephesus (AD 431).[26]

This tradition of the authority and trustworthiness of the
neighbourhood holy man who invariably produced the goods
seared itself deeply into the consciousness of the ordinary
people.[27] They preserved his memory and the sense of his
presence in a unique artistic form, known today as the icon.
Most icons preserved by the tradition of icon-painting to our
own day are of course not of local saints, but of the good and
the great in the Christian tradition, our Lady, St John the
Baptist, St George, and of the mysteries of the Trinity, the
Incarnation and the Assumption of the Virgin. But the icon
focuses on the person, the individual holy person, and in
itself reflects the value ordinary Christian worshippers place
on holy people with whom they can identify and on whose
prayers and intercession they can rely. The deeds, miracles
and wisdom of the saints hit the Byzantine tabloids much
more regularly than the decisions of councils or the *obiter dicta*
of the bishop, as indeed today a MORI poll asking the public
to name the most outstanding religious figures of our own
day would result in a list predominantly of lay people. Hence
the horror in the seventh century when the icons, by imperial

order, were piled on the bonfire and burned. Little did the authorities in church and state realise that what they were attacking was not popular superstition but lay authority, the self-authenticating authority of a holy life, the source of a wisdom that struck deep into the marrow of the realities of human existence. The iconoclasts failed; and the laity prevailed.[28]

The clergy however were still very much in place. The second century had seen the emergence of what we call today the 'historic threefold ministry'. By the beginning of the third century, Cornelius, Bishop of Rome, can write to Bishop Fabius of Antioch to say that at Rome in his time there were forty-six presbyters, seven deacons (presumably for the seven districts) and in addition these orders: seven sub-deacons, forty-two acolytes, fifty-two exorcists, readers and doorkeepers, and more than five hundred widows (who by this time constituted a special order in the church).[29] These are the so-called minor orders which have persisted in the western church to this day (and in the East which, since the Council *in Trullo* in 692, has retained lectors and cantors but has abolished doorkeepers, acolytes and exorcists).

Nothing is known of these in apostolic times (despite many attempts to prove their divine origin). They clearly came into being as the need arose, the subdeacons to assist the deacons, look after the sacred vessels, act as sidesmen and deliver official letters; the acolytes to carry tapers in the liturgy and act as general servants in the community; the lectors or readers to read the scriptures in church; the cantors to lead the singing; the doorkeepers to control the entrance to the church, a particularly tricky duty when each person's place in church had to be carefully observed, communicants in the front, catechumens in their own place, and penitents either at the back or not allowed in at all. Candidates for minor orders were not ordained by the laying-on of hands with prayer, but were appointed solemnly by the bishop, usually by means of a blessing and then the handing over to them of the instrument of their office (e.g. the paten to the subdeacon and the candlestick and candle to the acolyte).

The number of orders was not restricted to five and varies from region to region. But all those called to these offices were very definitely clergy,[30] and the practice arose of using these minor orders as a way of preparation for higher office in the Church. Athanasius, for example, was a reader in the church of Alexandria and actually lived with the bishop.[31] Augustine at Hippo, in the early years of his episcopate, established the custom of the clergy of the city living with him in his own house, a form of the common life which included the minor orders.[32] From this quasi-monastic seminary, bishops were regularly appointed to fill other sees as they fell vacant.[33] Eusebius of Vercelli had already done the same in his own diocese, and, at the end of the fourth century, Pope Siricius was to write to Himerius of Tarragona telling him that if he wanted more clergy then he should choose monks because their training and discipline in community had prepared them much better for the ordained ministry than a career in the world.[34] And as the years passed not only were monks ordained in order to serve local parishes and chantries, but even in the community itself monks were ordained to the priesthood, first (as has been recently shown)[35] to serve the many altars in the monastic church, but eventually, in some orders, almost as of right. By the time of Charlemagne society was more than generously provided with priests on whose services men and women of all ranks had come heavily to depend in their battle against the ever-threatening forces of evil. Bishops had become princes and, in the opinion of some, there was none higher under God than the Pope. For a time it seemed as if the human pilgrimage through this life, and the chances of escaping hell and gaining heaven in the next, lay entirely in the hands of the clergy.[36]

It is not surprising therefore that a severe check to such an illusion was imposed from time to time. Constantine may have freed the Church from fear of persecution; he may have promoted the influence of the Christian religion through reforms in the law and through active personal and financial support. But he never really forsook his pagan rôle as *pontifex maximus*, the great bridgemaker between society and the supernatural, the chief citizen charged with the task of preserving peace with the gods. This he simply carried over into his relationship with the Christian churches.[37] If it was he who promoted their interest, then it was he who would intervene to secure their unity and peace. It was the emperor, not bishops, who summoned councils. It was the emperor who ordered the exile of the unruly in order to promote greater peace. As bishops moved into the ranks of the *illustri* and the bishop of Rome acquired ceremonial privileges comparable to that of the emperor himself (e.g. the privilege of having his portrait hung during his reign)[38] so the state continued to make laws for and about the Church whose sole authority was the emperor through the civil courts.[39] Emperors were not above the Church's own internal discipline, as Theodosius found to his cost when, after having ordered the massacre of villagers in Thessalonica, he was greeted at the door of the church by St Ambrose and refused admission until he had done penance.[40] But none of this put the Church at the top of society's pyramid. Alcuin, writing to Charlemagne in 799, puts the record straight:

> There have so far been three positions in the world of the highest rank: that of the Pope, who is accustomed to rule the see of St Peter, the Prince of the Apostles, as his vicar . . . secondly, the Imperial dignity and secular power of the second Rome (i.e. Byzantium) . . . and thirdly, the royal dignity, in which the dispensation of our Lord Jesus Christ has placed you as the ruler of the Christian people, in power more excellent than the other two, in wisdom more distinguished, and the dignity of your rule more sublime. On you alone depends the whole safety of the Churches of Christ.[41]

Despite the very firm hold that monarchs in the middle ages retained over the totality of the affairs of Church and state, the power of the clergy remained unabated. As Christopher Brooke observes[42] there was during this period no more fundamental division in the whole of society than that between clergy and laity. Part of the reason was that the clergy were educated and the laity left mostly illiterate, including the nobility who were trained in the arts of war and

chivalry but not given much to reading or philosophy. When
William Burges, the Victorian decorative artist and lover of
the middle ages, was asked to decorate the interior of Cardiff
castle, he deemed that the prevailing interests of a mediaeval
baron when relaxing at home would be women and warfare,
and he painted accordingly. Scenes from classical mythology,
thought Burges, would be lost on a man who had probably
never opened a book. He was very close to the truth.[43] This
is in a way sad, because the mediaeval rulers of Church and
state were capable of creating great enthusiasms like the
Crusades on which thousands of lay people staked the salvation of their souls. But in the middle ages once more, as in
the early Church, it was holiness of life which brought
renewal to the Church and authority to the layman. It was
Franciscan poverty and literal conformity to the gospel which
endeared the friars to rich and poor alike. These men belonged to no hierarchy other than the simple one of their own
order. They could speak to the poor as equals, they themselves being poor. They could restore a dignity to men and
women trampled underfoot at the bottom of the social and
ecclesiastical pile. Small wonder that other lay movements
also appealed, mostly those which were later judged hereti-
cal, like the followers of Wycliff and John Hus, the Lollards
and the Waldensians, though in all these movements there
was another and more important factor involved, namely, the
steady filtering-through to lay people of the capacity to read
and write.[44]

The Renaissance when it came brought immense facilities
to those who now began to benefit from the revival in
learning. Schools as we know them were relatively few, but
upper-class laity, like Thomas More, were regularly tutored
in the houses of their contemporaries and then at the universities. Education, moreover, which included the critical
study of the church's literature, inevitably provoked challenges to the church's current stance and teaching in many
spheres. No longer was the church dependent on Peter
Lombard's extracts from the Fathers, when the Fathers
themselves could now be read in brand new editions printed

from a rich mine of new manuscripts. No longer could the
church be controlled in practice and teaching by Gratian's
summary of canon law, when the actual acts and deeds of the
great councils of the Church were now coming to light in the
collections of the patristic age. Perhaps most fundamentally
of all, the new critical editions of the Scriptures and their
translation into the vernacular were now hailed as the standard by which all Christian truth was to be measured. This
above all gave both reforming cleric and educated layman a
powerful instrument with which to challenge the assump-
tions of mediaeval christendom.[45]

But for all this, it was not the laity who wrote the theology
of the Reformation, nor the laity who activated the reforms.
Despite Luther's clear demonstration that Scripture declares all people to be God's priests (in which he was closely
followed by Calvin and John Knox), the Reformation remained a movement initiated and carried through by clerics
and princes. The latter of course were made very conscious
of their new responsibilities in the light of their breach with
the papacy and the development of national churches. In
England, for example, Thomas Bilson could observe that it
was no longer proper to speak of the king having temporal
authority and the church spiritual authority. In his view the
real distinction was between temporal and eternal authority.
Eternal power belonged to God, temporal power to the King
under God, and the church was confined purely to ordering
its own affairs in teaching, devotion and pastoral care under
the supervision of the Supreme Governor.[46] For this purpose,
the Convocations were allowed to continue meeting, but
only when summoned by the Sovereign at the opening of a
new Parliament.[47] So developed the doctrine of the godly
prince and the godly magistrate. And it has to be said that,
probably more by chance than determination, a genuine
attempt was made in the sixteenth century to credit at least
the laity in Parliament with the wisdom to conduct the affairs
of State according to the principles of the Christian religion.
The Book of Common Prayer in which this doctrine is so
clearly stated has probably achieved its longevity in part from

the fact that it is not merely a book for the church but a book for the nation. For its compilers remained convinced that true religion would only flourish if the King knew whose authority he had, if the Lords of the Council and all the nobility in carrying out their duties had grace, wisdom and understanding from above, and if the magistrates not only punished wickedness and vice but also sought to maintain true religion and virtue. In all these spheres, the layman was at the forefront of the Christian endeavour.

In the centuries that followed, King and Parliament continued to govern both church and state, and the one remaining ecclesiastical forum (the Convocations) in which the church might debate its own affairs was prorogued at the end of the eighteenth century, not to be summoned again until 1851. Clergy in the parishes were the subject of largely lay patronage. This was by no means always a disadvantage. Friendship with the patron and participation in his interests in the field and in local society could represent an affirmation of the life of the village and the estate as being consonant with the Christian religion and contributing to its furtherance. The parson who rode to hounds or the clergyman who played whist after dinner with the ladies he had encouraged to visit the poor and the sick were both in a sense affirming the laity in their ministry, though we have no record that they, the clergy, understood their work in this light.[48] All around them, of course, there grew an articulate laity who felt it increasingly their duty to bring Christian teaching into line with modern thought. It was the laity, most often, who took Scriptures and dogma by the scruff of the neck and subjected each to the scrutiny of reason. The result was sometimes alarming but by no means always disappointing. Voltaire was a great trailer of the coat, and his criticisms are sometimes on the verge of the obscene.[49] David Hume, however, remained a very godly man to his dying day and earned both respect and an audience for his skill in argument and sensitivity to his public.[50]

But any hope that the laity would take the lead in formulating theology is doomed to disappointment. Modern history has seen an immense increase in lay participation in church affairs, but very little solid affirmation of the lay person as such. In the Church of England, laity first became involved in church government in an advisory capacity when the Houses of Laity were added to the Convocations in the nineteenth century. The Enabling Act of 1919 was another landmark, setting up the Church Assembly and the whole system of Diocesan and Ruridecanal Conferences and Parochial Church Councils which again brought in lay people to manage church affairs at all levels on a scale never seen before. The General Synod, set up in 1969, seems to have set the seal on this whole process and stamped an authority on the lay voice in the church as having an equal partnership with that of the clergy, though not exactly on a level with the episcopate. By this account, many would say that the long reign of clerical domination is over and the laity have achieved at last their full and rightful place and voice in the church.[51]

Sadly this is not so. What has been created by this formal involvement of the laity in church consultations and decision making has been the professional lay person, the church, or even 'churchy', people, who are elected not simply for their quality as persons, but often on account of the lobby which they support. Thus for example, in the elections to General Synod in 1991, candidates all had to say where they stood in the matter of the ordination of women to the priesthood, and won or lost votes accordingly. And in Synod, much of their time and mental energy is taken up with debating the internal affairs of the church. The same is true in the parishes. Parishes duly elect a statutory number of men and women to the Parochial Church Council, but thereafter the debate in such councils is often and necessarily of a practical kind (about money, property etc.), though in fairness Parochial Church Councils do talk about worship, parish strategy, youthwork and other pastoral projects. Nonetheless, the debate is about the church and its work; and it is in this kind of arena that lay people are often seen to be contributing their work as the laity.

But it would be sad if the history of lay people in the church were to be told simply in terms of individuals or groups of lay people who, so to speak, 'did things for the church' and helped in its government, administration and in the planning of its strategy, or even 'substituted for the clergy' in teaching, preaching and pastoral care. To view the Synodsman or woman as the archetypal lay person is to lose a whole dimension of the understanding of the crucial rôle the laity play, not so much in the church but in the world. As Yves Congar observes, the Church, in the shape of its hierarchy, took many centuries to credit lay people with the leading rôle they have always played. This was partly because the standard of holy living was for so long set by the monastic orders, to which the secular clergy were certainly second best, and of which the laity were a poor and imperfect reflection. Life called apart from the world was in certain places and at certain times seen as superior to life in the secular order. And it was not until the thirteenth century, with the rediscovery of a philosophic realism, that the secular contribution of the laity was seen in a positive light. That the material world of nature and of commerce was a sphere to be valued, explored and treated with respect was a discovery that gave a whole new dimension to the understanding of the rôle of the laity. No longer were lay people hangers-on in the race to holiness, unlikely to succeed because they were (a) married and (b) embroiled in secular affairs. According to St Thomas, they were persons in their own right, not the lowest in a hierarchy of clergy, religious and laity, but fulfilling their own unique rôle in the mission of the Church, indeed at the very frontiers of its purposes.[52]

This is a concept of the lay person's calling which has probably succeeded in practice but has not always had theological or hierarchical backing. Protestantism, despite the 'work ethic', has frequently tended to divorce the lay person's personal religious life from the activities of the market place and the realities of its competitive nature. Catholicism too has made a bid for hearth and home without always grasping the real issues of work and society which influence every family belonging to a parish priest's care. Integrating movements, like the Christian Socialists, from the beginnings with F.D. Maurice to the developed concerns of the Christendom Group in the immediate post-war years, like (in some ways) *Action Catholique* in France, have made a brave attempt at saying that the structures of modern society are in themselves integrally important and that it is through these and not despite these that God works out his plan of salvation.[53] But the Church as a whole is not good at making these associations. It has a terrifying tendency to build a castle for the bishops and the lower clergy and to reserve a room in this for lay people, heavily conditioned by their involvement with the clergy, in order to discuss church matters, and then from this fortification to attempt to make their representations to the rest of humankind. It won't work. The laity do not need such formal involvement. The laity do not need authorising to do pastoral work in a parish. The laity have more than enough to do in fulfilling their calling. The laity firmly believe that they are the church in the front line, that they have unique opportunities that the clergy lack, and that theologically, they are as much the church as any other member. For in the last resort, it is the whole Church which is the instrument of God's purposes in the world, the whole Church which proclaims the truth in word and deed, the whole Church which leavens society and acts as a kind of benchmark in the human endeavour to distinguish between good and evil. The laity in other words are integral to the church's ministry; and the church has to learn that clerical leadership in certain and essential spheres of ecclesiastical life must be balanced by a proper recognition of lay leadership, lay expertise and lay responsibility in other areas. The Church after all is only incidental to God's purposes for the whole of creation. And what is needed today is a very strong affirmation of those who, each in their vocation and ministry, take the gospel into the darkest corners of human society where the clerical collar is an object of suspicion and ridicule, and where only the presence of sheer goodness and integrity represented by the laity can win the confidence of the doubting and fearful.

Notes

1. 1 Clement XL, 5.
2. See Hippolytus, *The Apostolic Tradition* 3, for the bishop as high priest and *Apostolic Constitutions* 2. 26.3, for the deacon as levite and presbyter as priest.
3. Clement of Alexandria, *Stromateis* 5.6.
4. R. de Vaux, *Ancient Israel* (ET London, 1961), pp. 70 ff.
5. Hosea 1: 9.
6. Hosea 2: 23.
7. 1 Peter 2: 9, 10.
8. Romans 9: 24–29.
9. Ephesians 2: 19–22.
10. 1 Peter 2: 9; Romans 15: 16 (the Greek text is here important).
11. Revelation 1: 6.
12. 1 Peter 2: 10.
13. See Excursus I, 'The origins of the episcopate' in my *The Authority of a Bishop* (London, 1987), pp. 76–84.
14. According to W.D. Davies, *St Paul and Rabbinic Judaism* (3rd edition, London 1970), pp. 56–57.
15. Isaiah 60, cf. Revelation 21.
16. 1 Cor. 15: 22; cf. Romans 5 on the first and second Adam.
17. 1 Cor. 12: 26.
18. 1 Cor. 12: 28–30; cf. Eph. 4: 11–16.
19. Luke 22: 24–27.
20. See S. Neil (ed.), *The Layman in Christian History* (London 1963), esp. chs. 1 and 2.
21. Cyprian, *The Lapsed, The Unity of the Catholic Church* translated and annotated by M. Bévenot (London 1957), ch. 2, p. 13 and nn. 4 and 17 pp. 78, 79. See also p. 28.
22. On the monks, see Derwas Chitty, *The Desert a City* (Oxford 1966).
23. Jerome, *Epistle* 52. 8 ff.
24. John Moschos, *De Vitis Patrum sive Patrum Spirituale*, MPL 74 cc. 19 ff.
25. John Rufus, *Plerophtheriae*, Patrologia Orientalis 13, p. 101. cit. P. Brown , *Society and the Holy* (London 1982), p. 158.
26. Theodoret, *Hist. Relig.* 26.

27. On the holy man in general, see P. Brown, 'The Rise and Function of the Holy Man in Late Antiquity', *Journal of Roman Studies* LXI (1971), pp. 80–101.

28. On the holy man and the iconoclastic controversy, see P. Brown, 'A Dark Age Crisis, Aspects of the Iconoclastic Controversy' in *English History Review* LXXXVIII (1973), pp. 1–34.

29. Cornelius, apud Eusebius, *Historia Ecclesiastica* VI.43.

30. J. Bingham, *The Antiquities of the Christian Church* (Oxford, 1855), Vol. 1 pp. 301 ff.

31. W. Robertson, Introduction to Nicene and Post–Nicene Fathers translation of *Select Works of St Athanasius*.

32. Augustine, *Sermo 355*.

33. Possidius, *Vita Sancti Augustini* XI ff.

34. Siricius, *Epistola 28* MPL LVI col.1361, 'Monachos quotque, quos tamen formam gravitatis et vitae ac fidei institutio sancta commendat, clerorum officiis aggregari et optamus et volumus.'

35. By A. Haussling, *Monchskonvent und Eucharistiefeier* (Munster 1973).

36. S. Neil, op. cit. pp. 88 ff.

37. See A. Alfoldi, *The Conversion of Constantine and Pagan Rome* (Oxford, 1948).

38. T. Klauser, *A Short History of the Western Liturgy* (ET. Oxford, 1969), pp. 32 ff.

39. As in the Theodosian and Justinian Codes, *passim*.

40. Ambrose, *Epistle 51*.

41. Alcuin, *Epistola 174* in Monumenta Germaniae Historica, 'Epistolae Karolini Aevi' II O 288.

42. In S. Neil, op. cit., pp. 111 ff.

43. See J. Mordaunt Crook, *William Burges and the Late Victorian Dream* (London, 1981), pp. 260–279.

44. S. Neil, op. cit., chapter 4 by C.N.L. Brooks. See also Ann Hudson, *The Premature Reformation* (Oxford, 1988).

45. Much of this is discussed in H.A. Enno van Gelder, *The Two Reformations in the Sixteenth Century* (The Hague, 1961).

46. This is reviewed in C. Morris, *Political Thought in England from Tyndale to Hooker* (Oxford, 1953).

47. On the Convocations, see T. Lathbury, *History of the Convocations of the Church of England* (London, 1842).

48. See, for example, I. Collins, *Jane Austen and the Clergy* (Hambledon Press, 1994).

49. As in the *Lettres Philosophiques* and more vulgarly in *Candide*.

50. See in particular his *Dialogues Concerning Natural Religion*.

51. See the Report, Church of England Archbishops' Commission, *Government by Synod* (London, 1966).
52. See Yves Congar, *Lay People in the Church* (London, 1957), pp. 32 ff. and *passim*.
53. 'The highest theology is most closely connected with the commonest practical life.' F.D. Maurice, *Acts of the Apostles* (1894, p. 315). 'I am convinced that theology will be a mere *hortus siccus* for Schoolmen to entertain themselves with, till it becomes associated once more with the Life of nations; that politics will be a mere ground on which despots and democrats and the tools of both play with the morality and happiness of their fellow-beings till we seek again for the ground of them in the nature and purposes of the eternal God.' ibid. *Gospel of St John* (1885), p. 315.

5

Ordination and Vocation

H.J.M. Turner

'According to traditional Catholic theology,' says *The Oxford Dictionary of the Christian Church*, 'the gift of Order is a Sacrament . . . Despite the various grades in the ministry it is agreed that there is but a single Sacrament of Orders. It is widely denied, however, that the orders lower than the diaconate can be reckoned a Sacrament.'[1] Somewhat differently, the Church of England boldly asserts, in the Preface to the Ordinal attached to the Book of Common Prayer, that 'it is evident unto all men diligently reading holy Scripture and ancient Authors, that from the Apostles' time there have been these Orders of Ministers in Christ's Church: Bishops, Priests, and Deacons', while in Article XXV it includes Orders as one of those 'commonly called Sacraments [which] are not to be counted for Sacraments of the Gospel'.

In conformity then with what is implied by the Preface, we shall not be speaking of 'a single Sacrament of Orders', nor need we discuss the exact sense in which ordination should be termed a sacrament. For our purpose in this chapter it is enough to insist that for Anglicans there is a real distinction between conferring holy orders upon a person and admitting him or her with due formality to a ministry officially recognised by the Church, for instance that of a reader. Ordination, like baptism, conveys what is in theological language called 'character' — once a priest always in some true sense a priest, even if unfrocked, just as once baptized always in some true sense a Christian, even if an apostate. Thus a valid baptism or a valid ordination cannot be repeated. It is therefore right to assert that bishops, priests and deacons are ordained primarily to be something rather than to perform certain duties, whereas a person is admitted as a reader in order to have authority to undertake the functions pertaining to that office.

But before we consider the ministries of the ordained, those who have been given a 'character', we must first allow Paul to remind us that in truth every Christian has a vocation to some form of ministry. In Romans 12: 4–8, and in 1 Corinthians 12: 4–31, he writes of the Church as the Body of Christ and insists that the various gifts (*charismata*) bestowed on the different members should be used for the good of the Body and should be accorded within it proper appreciation. Every Christian's initiation, by baptism, confirmation and communion, ought thus to be seen as at least potentially a vocation to some form of ministry. In this connection Hans Urs von Balthasar stresses the importance of confirmation: 'The personal mission bestowed by the Holy Spirit is linked to the sacrament of confirmation by which the Christian is raised from a life that was predominantly the receptive and irresponsible life of a child to one that has a voice and responsibility within the ecclesial community.'[2]

Having been reminded that each member of the Church has a vocation, we can hardly avoid discussing hierarchy and status. Are the ordained better Christians than the remainder of the laity? Does the title 'reverend' imply higher status? And does a hierarchy of bishops, priests, deacons conflict with our Lord's words, 'You have one teacher, and you are all brethren'?[3]

In 1 Corinthians 12 there comes in verse 28 a list of ministers presented in the form of a hierarchy: 'God has appointed in the Church first apostles, second prophets, third teachers . . .' But earlier, in verses 22–25, when writing of the human body, which he uses as a picture of the Church, Paul has insisted that 'the parts of the body which seem to be weaker are indispensable . . . God has so adjusted the body, giving the greater honour to the inferior part, that there may be no discord in the body . . .' The humblest Christians at Corinth, therefore, were to feel that in fulfilling whatever ministries they were called to undertake, they were no less essential than the apostles to the proper functioning of the Church. At the same time there was, of course, no doubt in Paul's mind that he himself was an apostle,[4] and that he had the right and duty to exercise authority over the Corinthian Church,[5] with a view to the 'building up' of its members.[6]

Nevertheless in the light of his assertion that every member of the Church is to be respected as exercising a ministry, Paul would scarcely have approved of giving the title 'reverend' to certain only among them; he would undoubtedly have denied that, merely in virtue of the ministry to which he has been called, one Christian is a better or more prestigious Christian than another; and although Paul did put apostles at the top of a seemingly hierarchical list, he wrote also, 'I think that God has exhibited us apostles as last of all, like men sentenced to death.'[7] It is not perhaps a serious matter if the ordained are styled 'reverend', but it is regrettable that many in the Church of England do cling to mistaken ideas about the status conferred by ordination. It is still largely true, as years ago Bishop John Robinson put it, that:

> Nothing . . . is more deeply entrenched in our society than what I have called 'the Clergy line' . . . Yet, of course, it was not a primitive division in the Church . . . The early Church knew . . . a very great diversity of ministries within the Body . . . There was every conceivable contribution of ministry and liturgy to the life of the early Church — from each man according to his ability. And yet, there is no evidence that at any one point within this diversity a line was drawn above which, as it were, came those with dog-collar status and below which came the laity.[8]

It was probably in part a result of Christianity's becoming in the fourth century the official religion of the Roman empire that the Church's ministerial hierarchy came to be thought of as a sort of parallel to the *cursus honorum* by which those seeking high office in the state ascended from one magistracy to another. Ideas of this kind underlie the prayer found in the Ordinal attached to the Book of Common Prayer that the newly-ordained deacons 'may so well behave themselves in this inferior Office that they may be found worthy to be called unto the higher Ministries in [God's] Church'. In much of Europe the false emphasis on the distinction between clergy and laity also owes a good deal to the fact that for centuries those in orders were literate, while most lay people were not. Yet, whether or not people were conscious of a 'clergy line', original sin ensured that the Church from New Testament times onwards was not free from authoritarianism, hierarchical notions of the wrong sort, and the desire for status: thus already in 1 Peter 5: 3 the elders (presbyters) had to be reminded to minister 'not as domineering over those in your charge'; in 3 John 9f. we read of 'Diotrephes, who likes to put himself first', and who may have been 'the first "monarchical bishop" known to history in the province of Asia',[9] and, to take an example from the third century, Paul of Samosata, Bishop of Antioch, was accused not only of heresy but also of having excessive honours paid to himself, including the singing of his praises on Easter day.

If the people of God could be brought to recognise and resist the attractions which clericalism has, both for the ordained and, in a different way, for the unordained, this would be a step towards gaining a right understanding of what a vocation to diaconate, priesthood or episcopate really involves. In addition to 1 Corinthians 12, a key passage is Luke 22: 26f., 'Let the greatest among you become as the youngest, and the leader as one who serves . . . I am among you as one who serves'. These are some of Christ's words at the Last Supper, significantly uttered in the context of a dispute about prestige, 'which of [the disciples] was to be regarded as the greatest'. Let us bear in mind that the Greek word underlying 'serves' is that from which we get 'deacon' in English, and a literal translation would be, '. . . the leader as one who deacons . . . I am among you as one who deacons.'

On the one hand, then, Paul teaches us that every Christian has a vocation to a ministry of some kind in the Church, and that no ministry ought to be thought of as 'inferior', while on the other hand ministers, ordained or not, are reminded by our Lord that their vocation is, like his, a vocation to service. But if 'to each [member] is given the manifestation of the Spirit for the common good',[10] and if all ministries have the same ultimate purpose, the upbuilding of Christ's Body in love,[11] what is so distinctive about three ministries that they are called holy orders and are conferred by an admission ceremony that is at least akin to a sacrament, ordination?

We remarked earlier that bishops, priests, and deacons are ordained primarily to be something and secondarily to perform certain duties. The ordained then may be described as 'signs'. Now it is to be noted that the Orthodox, the Roman Catholic and the Anglican Churches first ordain to the diaconate candidates who may subsequently become priests or bishops. Furthermore if either or both of the so-called 'higher' orders are additionally conferred upon them they do not cease to be deacons. The diaconate, because of our Lord's words, is a 'sign' which declares to the Church and to the world the true nature of every Christian ministry. And this diaconal mark is not to be absent from those ministries whose holders may have to exercise something akin to what Paul called 'the authority which the Lord has given me', the purpose of which, he added, is 'for building up and not for tearing down'.[12] As I wrote elsewhere:

> Even if, as is sometimes said today, there is really no liturgical or other duty performed by a deacon which lay persons may not also be permitted to undertake, deacons are needed because, by the fact of their having been solemnly ordained, they signify the Church's perpetual determination to view all forms of ministry as a sharing in the diaconate of Christ.[13]

A distinctive ordained diaconate is not an optional extra.

The episcopate similarly is intended primarily to be a 'sign': the bishop in his person is to unite the church in the diocese with the Catholic Church which extends throughout the centuries and (ideally) throughout the whole world, while within his diocese the bishop is meant to be personally the focus of unity. It is hardly necessary to say that divisions between Christian Communions frustrate these intentions, though this does not mean that the episcopate should be abandoned, but rather that the search for Christian unity must never be given up.

As regards the priesthood, otherwise styled the presbyterate, one cannot so easily speak of a single 'sign'. This is because the priesthood has become something different from what it originally was, a council of presbyters (elders), associated with the bishop in the pastoral care and government of the local church. Early in the second century, Ignatius of Antioch in one of his letters compared the priests to the council of the apostles;[14] in the early third century Hippolytus' liturgy, in the prayer at the ordination of priests, contains the petition, 'Look upon this Thy servant and impart to him the spirit of grace and counsel that he may share in the presbyterate and govern Thy people with a pure heart'.[15] However, as the number of congregations grew, and the local bishop became unable personally to preside over every Eucharist in each church in what we should now call his diocese, he began to delegate to individual priests some of his responsibilities, entrusting congregations to their immediate care.

The Greek Orthodox theologian John Zizioulas has emphasised the significance of this change:

> What the emergence of the parish did was to destroy this [existing] structure, a destruction which affected not only the episcopal office but also that of the presbyter. For it meant that from then on the eucharist did not require the presence of the presbyters as a *college* . . . An *individual* presbyter was thus enough to create and lead a eucharistic gathering — a parish. Could that gathering be called 'Church'?[16]

Priests have thus come to undertake many of a bishop's liturgical functions, including especially that of presiding at the Eucharist. Hence in the eyes of most Roman Catholics and Anglicans priesthood has for long been seen as the normal example of ordained ministry. Hence too a parish priest, acting under the authority of a bishop and as his deputy, has in some ways as a 'sign' differed little from a bishop, though having a more limited sphere. Nevertheless, if in a diocesan synod, instead of the current distinction between the laity on the one hand and the clergy, including deacons, on the other, the priests were specifically associated with the bishop as his advisers, they would then be seen collectively as a 'sign' of the union of monarchical and collegiate elements in church government.

The functions or duties of the ordained flow from what they are, through the 'character' bestowed in ordination. And Anglicans should have no doubt that ordination, whether it is or is not reckoned a sacrament, bestows power and authority as well as 'character', for our liturgy assumes that these have been conveyed to those ordained to the priesthood. Accordingly, in the Book of Common Prayer the congregation at Matins and Evensong is expressly told that God 'hath given power and commandment, to his Ministers, to declare and pronounce to his people, being penitent, the Absolution and Remission of their sins'. Significantly the word 'power' was omitted from the nineteenth-century Methodist version of Morning Prayer.[17] In the same way whereas the immediately preceding rubric in the Prayer Book states that the Absolution is 'to be pronounced by the Priest alone', the Methodist wording at that point speaks of 'A Declaration as to the Forgiveness of Sins, to be made by the Minister'. Anglicanism thus reveals liturgically something of what it believes about the function and power of a priest, while the Methodists, of course, revised the service in order to demonstrate that according to their theology of ordination a minister has simply been entrusted with a duty to perform.

In Anglicanism, then, ordination is held both to confer 'character', so that the ordained may be 'signs', and also to give them power, so that they may perform the functions which belong to their order. But everything possible should be done to eliminate the spurious *mystique* often attached to the priesthood, which, as we have said, is in the eyes of many the normal type of ordained ministry. In opposition to this, church people ought often to be reminded that at the Eucharist the priest merely 'lends his tongue and provides his hand', as John Chrysostom said.[18] The *mystique* may be partly the result of what John Robinson called 'the clergy line' separating the ordained from the laity; at the same time, since in England to-day the clergy are far less respected by the general public than were their predecessors in the past, it may also be due in part to the desire of the ordained to enhance their status in the eyes of their fellow-churchmen by an emphasis on 'my vocation'. After ordination one is, it is true, in holy orders, but this does not imply artificial separation from one's fellow-Christians, or from the world and from what is entailed by living in it. The vocation to be ordained should be recognised, both by ordinands and others, as very different from a call either to be a prophet, or to embrace the religious life as a monk, friar or nun. The call to be a bishop, or priest, or deacon, should be looked at in a matter of fact way: the Church needs ministers, and it calls to ordination those of its members who appear to possess, at least potentially, the qualities which a bishop, a priest, or a deacon will require.

A welcome indication that some in the Church of England are beginning to think along these lines has been given in the bishops' *Guidelines for Local Non-Stipendiary Ministry* (ACCM 1987) and in *Call to Order* (1989), the report of an ACCM Working Party. Unfortunately, all too often such productions and the ideas they contain appear too upsetting to be taken seriously, as seems to have occurred in the case of *Deacons in the Ministry of the Church* (GS 802, 1988). So an approach to vocation to ministry along the lines sketched in the preceding paragraph, and clearly found in the first two publications just mentioned, will have to contend with an unquestioning assumption that the call to be ordained is just like that to be a religious or a prophet, and comes in the same way.

The Bible gives examples of the vocation to be a prophet coming as a direct personal call from God — Amos, Isaiah, and Jeremiah spring to mind.[19] The calls to Antony of Egypt and to Francis of Assisi came through their suddenly realising that words from the Bible which they heard read in church were personally addressed to them by God.[20] By responding, Antony became the pioneer of monasticism and Francis the inaugurator of a movement which became the Order of Friars Minor. Although it is true that in former ages people have been forced to enter monasteries or convents as a result of political or family pressure, neither the Church nor any of its members can give anybody a genuine vocation to be a prophet or become a religious. A true call to prophesy or to enter the religious life, whatever circumstances bring it to a person's consciousness, is one that comes from God and is received and recognised internally.

Being called to any of the three ordained ministries of the Church is, however, a different matter. As against what is usually taken for granted nowadays, for many centuries the Church considered an inwardly-felt desire to be ordained not a *prima facie* mark of a vocation, but a contra-indication. The *Life* of Hugh, Bishop of Lincoln (born *c.* 1140), provides a good illustration of what was hagiographically and thus traditionally thought to be right and proper:

> When Hugh was barely eight years old his father, a widower, joined a community of canons regular near Grenoble and brought the boy with him as an oblate. In his nineteenth year Hugh was ordained deacon . . . in response to the demands of his brethren, though much against his own will. Then, attracted by the greater strictness of the rule followed at the Grande Chartreuse, he moved there and joined the Carthusian Order. After some years, the monk who was his director told him that, if he wished, he might now be ordained priest. He replied that there was nothing in his life that he more desired, and this answer horrified the older man. 'What is this that you have said?' he exclaimed. 'Who would have believed that you could be so presumptuous or could say that? What an appalling thing! You have so often read the words, He who comes to the priesthood otherwise than unwillingly, comes unworthily, and yet, as you confess, you are unafraid of coming to it, not unwillingly, but even eagerly'.[21]

We are not concerned with the remainder of Hugh's story, but we ought to ponder the implications both of the way in

which he received his vocation to the diaconate, and also
of the older monk's reaction on hearing of a desire to be
priested.

Similar testimony to an understanding of the summons to
ordination as coming normally from without to a reluctant
candidate is found in the liturgical practice of the Eastern
Orthodox Churches: at an ordination, the future deacon or
priest is led forward to the bishop by two members of the
clergy who hold his arms, a reminder of the need in earlier
times to prevent an escape on the part of someone whom the
Church was calling to be ordained, but who might try to run
away from his vocation.

The evidence shows that for a very long period throughout
the Church it was indeed regarded as normal for a vocation
to come through a man's being invited or urged to be ordained by a congregation or by a superior, and there are
instances of the employment of a horrifying degree of com-
pulsion. Why then is it now widely assumed that a call to
ordination does not come from without, maybe to the reluctant, but that, if genuine, it resembles that to the religious
life, and is felt internally as a desire or a prompting?

Already in the Ordinal attached to the Book of Common
Prayer, those to be ordained deacon are asked: 'Do you trust
that you are inwardly moved by the Holy Ghost to take upon
you this Office and Ministration . . . ?', although this question is not repeated at the ordination of deacons to the
priesthood. In the *Alternative Service Book* however, in both
cases the ordinands have the question put to them: 'Do you
believe, so far as you know your own heart, that God has
called you to the office and work of a deacon [or priest] in
his Church?'. In this form there is some relief for those
troubled by inner doubts, but the implication is still that an
internal call constitutes a vocation. One can only speculate
as to why Cranmer introduced the question into the Ordinal,
but it may be that he believed the authority for the institution of the diaconate to come from the account in Acts 6,
where we read that, *before* the apostles laid hands on the
Seven, one of the requirements was that the chosen candi-

dates should be 'full of the Spirit'.[22] It is possible that Cranmer held that this ought to be true of those about to become Anglican deacons, and that they too should be conscious of the Spirit's indwelling.[23]

The suppression of the monasteries may also have contributed something to the widespread acceptance in England of the assumption that a call to ordination is an internal matter. In the western church there had for a long time been a tendency to assimilate, so far as possible, the obligations of the secular clergy to those of the religious — the requirement of celibacy is an obvious example. An internal vocation, which is properly expected in the case of those called to be monks or friars, could thus already have been thought by some to be a proper qualification for holy orders as well. And when there were no longer any monks or friars, it is not surprising if some men who were conscious of being called to express publicly their Christian commitment saw ordination as the natural way to do so. As a perceptive priest has written, 'The bulk of laymen who are serious about religion at some point consider the possibility of ordination . . .'[24] This is because even today, while all Anglicans think they know what it means to be ordained, many still regard the religious life as something so exotic that they cannot envisage the possibility that it is to this that they are being called.

But the Church of England is not the only church which since the sixteenth century has come to expect an internal vocation to be the normal prelude to ordination. In France, for example, for reasons into which we need not now enter, there was a growing tendency after the Counter-Reformation to look for 'the essence of priestly vocation in the feelings, inclinations and dispositions of the individual candidate'. This 'attraction theory', as it came to be known, 'finally went so far as to assert that the candidate who believed he could lay claim to the possession of such an attraction had the right to receive holy orders, that is the right to demand that he be admitted to the priesthood'.[25] Later some opposition developed in France, but in the nineteenth century this view was widely held, and Anglo-Catholics in contact with the French church probably met it, and were thus confirmed in the understanding or misunderstanding of vocation which they already had.

It is worth quoting here what the Jesuit director of vocations for Britain wrote a few years ago: 'Many, if not most, who show interest in becoming a priest reply that they do not really want to, but that they feel they are being asked to. The Lord is perceived as "nagging" them to become a priest or follow a religious vocation.'[26] This is very interesting, for it reveals both a continuing failure to distinguish between the vocation to the religious life and that to ordination, and also the consequent persistence of the 'attraction theory' as regards the latter, even though it is now stated that the internal prompting may be felt as a nagging rather than a desire.

In France, in a book published in 1909, J. Lahitton strove to reassert a more theological basis for the call to ordination. He pointed out that 'if candidates for the priesthood possess the vocation to it in themselves, they could demand ordination as a right'. Accordingly he maintained that 'when a person is called to the priesthood by the Church's legitimate ministers, this calling does not assume the existence in him of a vocation, but it is the calling itself which creates the vocation in him'. He rejected, however, any idea of conscription, for the ordaining bishop 'officially invites [the ordinands] to receive the order for which they have been chosen . . . This vocation is officially and clearly *proposed*, it is not *imposed*.'[27]

The publication by Lahitton of his book led to disputes within the Roman Catholic Church, but 'a commission formed by Pius X decided, on all essential points, in favour of [his] thesis'. However, having acknowledged this, von Balthasar cautiously added that 'it is clear to-day that the commission's decision was not intended to question the existence of an inner calling (as Lahitton did with his exaggerated views), but only to affirm that the "feeling" of being called carried with it no right to ordination so far as the Church was concerned . . .'[28]

Following Lahitton and adopting a similar stance another French priest, Abbé Long-Hasselmans, came to see that one must speak not only of the Church's call to individuals, but also of demands made on a parish with regard to the quality of its Christian life. The right to tell one or more of its members that they should take seriously an invitation to be ordained depends, he said, on the existence of 'a united and fervent community, conscious of the privileges which baptism has conferred on all its members; a Christian community which really is Christ's mystical Body, having the duty and the right to participate in him and to continue his priestly offering'.[29]

The theological ideas of Lahitton and Long-Hasselmans can be shown to be in harmony with Christian tradition, but it would be idle to pretend that they are other than demanding. That, however, is not to say that the Church can safely neglect them in favour of what appears more 'practical'.

In the area of vocations to the religious life, a vocation is rightly understood as an inner urge, whatever prompted it, and whether it is experienced as a desire or a nagging. It is the genuineness of this feeling that must of course be tested. When it concerns one of the Church's ministries, whether ordained or officially authorised, the concept of vocation is different. As regards the episcopate, this is generally accepted, for we should be shocked if, because of some internal prompting, a man went around saying, 'I'm sure I have a vocation to be a bishop'. Instructed Anglicans ought also to experience a sense of shock if they hear a person, male or female, proclaim on the basis of an inner feeling, 'I'm sure I have a vocation to be a priest' (or 'to be a deacon'). The 'attraction theory' is unsound. Whether or not it is right to ordain women to the priesthood, the Church's traditional understanding of vocations to ordained ministry denies the force of claims originating from internal convictions, however sincerely felt.

Furthermore, rejection of the 'attraction theory' would make it easier to select ordinands. Those responsible for interviewing candidates would no longer have to assess the authenticity of individuals' claims to have experienced an inner call — a hard task for selectors who meet candidates only for a short time, unlike the members of a religious community when assessing a postulant's vocation. The selectors, on the basis of their knowledge of the Church's current need for ministers, both ordained and unordained, would simply try to discern the suitability, actual or potential, of those who had accepted an invitation to present themselves with the possibility of being recommended for some form of ministry. There would be no need to thrust aside insensitively those claiming to feel an internal vocation to some form of ministry, provided they could be brought to understand that the Church always has the right and duty to determine both what ministers it requires at any given time, and also to which ministry any volunteers should, if accepted, be assigned. Perhaps too, if the true nature of a vocation to ordained or authorised ministry were more widely understood, there would be a better chance of more men and women recognising that in reality they were being called to the religious life.

In his recent book, *The Shape of the Ministry*, Canon M.A.H. Melinsky specifically notes that an analogous method of selection for local non-stipendiary ministry 'is in sharp contrast with the traditional Anglican idea of vocation as an inner call experienced by the individual and then tested by the Church'.[30] He does not draw attention to the principle involved in this method. But if it is accepted as right that 'the call of God to [local non-stipendiary] ministry comes to the candidate, in the first place, through the local congregation of which the individual is a member . . .',[31] ought not the same principle to apply to all vocations? If not, we are in danger of rejecting Paul's teaching by instituting a hierarchy of ministerial status, with the local non-stipendiary priest so low in it that his vocation is assumed to be quite different from that of other priests of a higher class.

It is vital that, as regards every priest, the truth be recognised that he 'is not a man who stands between us and God, but a man who stands out of the way from between us and

God'.[32] But acknowledging that all have received the same character should not lead us to insist that every priest must perform precisely the same functions as every other priest, and this applies also to deacons and bishops. Therefore there should be variations in the training given, both before and after ordination, to those who have accepted the Church's call to be ordained. Training needs to be devised to fit them for those kinds of ministry which the Church perceives to be required, and for which the individual ordinands have shown themselves to possess the necessary gifts, whether actually or potentially.

As an example let us consider how this might operate in the light of the need in many places for pastorally-minded eucharistic presidents. There are doubtless not a few men respected by their fellow-worshippers and fully able to undertake a pastoral and liturgical ministry, but with no gift for preaching. These, if willing to accept the vocation, could be given appropriate training, taught how to conduct worship and to preside at the Eucharist, and first ordained to the diaconate and then to the priesthood. But they should not be forced to try to become preachers, if their Maker never intended them to occupy the pulpit.

It is sad that for many years a very different policy has been adopted in the Church of England. We have noted the acceptance of the 'attraction theory'. It is also necessary to remember that, after the Reformation, the preaching of sermons came to be seen as the most important function of ordained ministers, and thus the aim was to secure a learned preacher in every parish. This ideal was never realised, but it exercised great influence when the training of ordinands was being considered, perhaps most conspicuously in 1909 when the bishops of the Province of Canterbury decided that from 1917 all ordinands should have both a university degree and at least one year's theological, practical and devotional training. The first world war made it impossible to implement the plan, which anyhow would probably not have been a success. The sad thing is that little attention was paid to the problem of how the Church of England in the twentieth century ought to seek to communicate to its members the essentials of the Christian faith. This problem has been with us for at least three generations, and it is now surely obvious that it will not be solved by sermons, even if we were to be given a supply of candidates conscious of an internal vocation and also capable of becoming learned preachers. But in all this time we have not called to the priesthood many who in other respects would have made admirable priests and pastors.

In this chapter I have touched on many important and controversial matters. I am well aware that my treatment of them has been sketchy, but I hope that I may have succeeded in questioning some presuppositions. My plea is that currently accepted ideas, which are held unthinkingly, be subjected to renewed theological scrutiny, in the light of Christian history as a whole. Some churches may spend too much time arguing about the minutiae of theology; the Church of England, however, would have been more practically effective over the last hundred years if it had given as much thought to the *theology* of ordination and vocation as it has to matters of finance and organization.

Notes

1. op. cit., 'Orders and Ordination'.
2. Hans Urs von Balthasar, *The Christian State of Life* (San Francisco, 1983), p. 331.
3. Matt. 23: 8.
4. 1 Cor. 9: 1.
5. e.g. 1 Cor. 4: 14–21.
6. 2 Cor. 10: 8.
7. 1 Cor. 12: 28 ; 4: 9.
8. John A.T. Robinson, *Layman's Church* (London, 1963), pp. 10 f.
9. C.H. Dodd, *The Johannine Epistles* (London, 1945), p. 164.
10. 1 Cor. 12: 7.
11. Eph. 4: 16.
12. 2 Cor. 13: 10.
13. H.J.M. Turner, *Ordination and Vocation — Yesterday and Today* (Worthing, 1990), p. 57.
14. *Magnesians*, 6.
15. *The Apostolic Tradition of St Hippolytus* 6. (In Dix, re-issued by H. Chadwick, 1968) viii, 2, p. 13.

16. J.D. Zizioulas, *Being as Communion* (New York, 1985), p. 250. Further thought is needed about the effect which the emergence of the parochial system had on the ministries of bishops and priests. Was the system adopted as a mere expedient, with no theological thinking as to what it meant for the Church's ministries? If so, what are the implications for the Church to-day?

17. *The Book of Public Prayers and Services for the Use of the People Called Methodists [as adopted by the Conference of 1882]*

18. PG 59: 72.

19. Amos 7: 14 f.; Isaiah 6: 1–8; Jeremiah 1: 4–10.

20. Antony — Matt. 19: 21; Francis — Matt. 10: 7 ff.

21. H.J.M. Turner, op. cit., p. 28, quoting Adam of Eynsham, *Magna Vita Sancti Hugonis*, eds. D.L. Douie and D.H. Farmer (Oxford Medieval Texts, 2nd edn 1985), I. Bk. I. chs. iv and xi.

22. Acts 6: 3.

23. cf. P.F. Bradshaw, *The Anglican Ordinal*, Alcuin Club Collections 53 (London, 1971), pp. 34 f.

24. R.E.C. Browne, *Love of the World* (Worthing, 1986), p. 138.

25. W. Stockums (tr. J.W. Grundner), *Vocations to the Priesthood* (London, 1937), pp. 30 f.

26. D. Birchall, *The Tablet*, 15 Aug. 1987, p. 869.

27. J. Lahitton, *La Vocation Sacerdotale* (Paris, 1909), pp. 43, 33, 92 (italics his).

28. von Balthasar, op. cit., pp. 443, 445.

29. B. Emonet, summary of a speech by Long-Hasselmans, *Etudes*, 189 (5 Dec. 1926), p. 540.

30. M.A.H. Melinsky, *The Shape of the Ministry*, (Norwich, 1992) p. 239, referring to *Guidelines for Local Non-Stipendiary Ministry*, p. 237.

31. *Guidelines . . .*, p. 237. It is noteworthy that the Bishop of Salisbury has decided to try to find some 200 local non-stipendiary clergy, according to *The Times*, 18 October 1994. The article does not describe their exact duties or their training.

32. P.N. Waggett, SSJE, *The Holy Eucharist* (London, 1906), p. 23.

6

Function and Profession

Peter Davie

Most Anglican parish churches display a board listing the names of the incumbents of the living from the Middle Ages down to the present day. Such a list of names might well furnish an outline history of the Church of England in a local setting, for it is in the story of its parishes and of the priests who served them that the heart of the church's history is to be discovered. The aim of the present essay is to outline one aspect of that story. It describes how clergy have exercised their distinctive functions and acquired a professional status since the Reformation, and concludes with a discussion a about the future of a professional ministry.

I

It was at the Reformation that a functional idea of the ordained ministry came to the fore in the Church of England.[1] In the late Middle Ages there were many priests such as members of religious orders, those who served chantries, teachers, lawyers or administrators, who rarely if ever performed any clerical function other than that of celebrating Mass. Although the many manuals published for the guidance of late-medieval parish priests indicate that for some clergy at least their priestly functions were not restricted to saying Mass — they were called to counsel penitents, teach children and to prepare the dying for their journey into the next world — there was, nevertheless, a widespread tendency for priests to focus upon one function, that of celebrating the Mass, and for the clergy to become a sacerdotal caste isolated from the laity.

The Reformation of the sixteenth century initiated crucial changes in the understanding and practice of the ordained ministry in the Church of England designed to rectify abuses and distortions in the priesthood. As in other Reformed Churches, the ordained minister was no longer regarded as possessing a superior status within the Church. It was recognised that baptism marked the moment of entry into priestly ministry. The ordained ministry was not abolished, but there were fundamental changes in the understanding of its nature and functions. The ordained minister was now thought of as one called and set aside at ordination to perform a broad set of functions on behalf of the whole priestly body, which were no longer restricted to one task in isolation. The minister was charged with a wide range of tasks, all of which were concerned with the communication of God's word as revealed in Jesus Christ — preaching, teaching, spiritual guidance and the administration of the sacraments.

The clergy now constituted a more homogeneous body of men. Prior to the Reformation, as we have seen, many priests lived and worked outside the parochial system. Subsequently, with the destruction of the monasteries and chantries, together with the secularisation of the law, education and administration, there were few openings for clergymen other than in parish work.

Early in Elizabeth I's reign it became evident that there was an urgent need to recruit a body of ministers better able to perform the more demanding tasks of the reformed ministry. The Queen's bishops attempted to increase the number of clergy and to improve their quality; they looked to the schools and universities to achieve these aims for them. On the Continent the Council of Trent had recently attempted to raise priestly standards by decreeing that a seminary to train priests was to be set up in every diocese.

All the churches, whether Protestant or Catholic, sought to enhance the quality of preaching and teaching offered by their priests and ministers. A man might be able to stumble through the Mass with a smattering of Latin, but he would not be able to dispel superstition or instruct his flock in Christian faith and practice without adequate education. In its doctrinal decrees aimed at countering Protestantism, the Council of Trent reiterated the medieval emphasis on the priestly offering of the eucharistic sacrifice, but in its decrees on practical reforms it also raised the status of preaching as a priestly function.[2] The aim of all the churches was to produce ordained ministers who would be more effective pastors and teachers than many of their predecessors had been.

By 1630 the grammar schools and universities were successfully producing the educated men the bishops of the Church of England required for their parishes. The clergy could now be described as a profession. Some historians have argued that this development did not occur until the nineteenth century when the clergy adopted a model provided by the new secular professions that were then coming into being. It is more plausible to suggest, however, that what the nineteenth century witnessed was a revival of an earlier development that had already taken place in the first third of the seventeenth century.[3]

George Herbert's *The Country Parson*, a classical work in the literature of Anglican pastoral theology, was composed at the beginning of the 1630s as Herbert prepared himself to take on the cure of souls at Bemerton near Salisbury.[4] It is not a simple description of practice, but rather an outline of the ideals he proposed should guide him in his work as a parish priest. Even so, it may be taken as a reliable account of the functions and ideals of a parish priest at the time, as I have argued, at which the Anglican clergy became recognizable as a body of professionals.

Herbert's parson is concerned about every aspect of his parishioners' lives, secular as well as religious. In order to help them he studies books on law and medicine; he even concerns himself with veterinary matters. Nevertheless his chief concern is the spiritual welfare of his flock. His aim is to establish a living Christian community in his parish centred upon constant teaching and daily worship in the village church.

Herbert's parson is above all a teacher. As a pastor and teacher he is charged with rescuing his flock from error and leading them to obey God's word, not merely through words, but also through personal example in all aspects of his life, domestic as well as public.

The parson's chief function is to communicate the word of God to his people. He is to preach 'constantly', for 'the pulpit is his joy and his throne'.[5] When he preaches he is to use all suitable means to gain attention, such as 'earnestness of speech', and taking care to direct his remarks to the different groups in the congregation, the young and the old, the rich and the poor. Like most of his contemporaries, Herbert had been trained in rhetoric at university. He later taught the subject for a while at Cambridge. It is no surprise then that he emphasises the importance of persuasive speech in the pulpit.

Preaching is best suited, he declares, to 'inflaming' the 'knowledge of salvation' already implanted in the minds of a flock by regular catechizing at Evening Prayer on Sunday afternoons. This practice is to be esteemed not merely because its use is enjoined in the Prayer Book and Canons, but also because it is the ideal way of teaching. Indeed the use of its question-and-answer method should extend beyond the set questions to testing pupils with questions of the parson's own devising, after the manner of Socrates with his pupils in Athens. The exercise should be of use also to parents and other adults who witness it, as an opportunity to revise and extend their knowledge of the Christian faith.

Yet the parson's chief concern is not with the techniques of teaching or with rhetoric, important as these are. His main aim must be to deepen and expand his own knowledge and understanding of the Christian faith. The 'chief and top' of his study must be to gain knowledge of 'the Holy Scriptures'.

Herbert contends that no external ecclesiastical guide is
needed in the devout reading of Scripture. The danger of
succumbing to a merely subjective interpretation of the
sacred text may be avoided if the rules laid down by the
Reformers are duly observed. The devout reader must approach God's word in full reliance upon prayer and the
guidance of the Holy Spirit. Also one part of Scripture should
be interpreted in the light of others, and discriminating use
made of commentaries, especially those of the Fathers. Out
of all this reading and pondering the parson should compile
'a book and a body of Divinity' as a source for his prayer and
teaching.[6]

The parson's ultimate aim is to build up a worshipping
community. The strong emphasis upon preaching and teaching among both Protestants and Catholics at this time had
its origin in a desire to move congregations on from merely
external participation in rites and ceremonies to an intelli-
gent inner participation in worship. Herbert is also concerned that any deepening of his parishioners' spiritual lives
should not take the subjective turn of some tendencies in
the spirituality of the time which encouraged introspection
and individualism. Herbert's aim is to root personal devotion
in communal worship. The parson's own spiritual life is to be
rooted in the regular, communal recitation of Morning and
Evening Prayer in church, in which the laity are to be urged
to join. On Sundays the same pattern is to be repeated with
the addition of a sermon in the morning and the Catechism
in the afternoon. Holy Communion is to be celebrated at
least five or six times a year and ideally once a month. Thus
teaching is to lead the flock to regular devout participation
in the communal acts of parish worship.

At the beginning of this century, in a pioneering attempt
to introduce a scientific approach to pastoral theology, Clement Rogers reviewed the Anglican tradition of pastoral theology
and accused Herbert of amateurism.[7] *The Country Parson*
lacked a theoretical basis and rested upon mere haphazard
observations. Such a judgement is wide of the mark. As we
have seen, Herbert's directives on preaching and teaching

have a complex, if briefly stated, theoretical underpinning. Biblical exegesis is to be based upon carefully formulated principles of interpretation; persuasive exposition is to be based upon humanistic principles of rhetoric. Herbert was no mere amateur. His view of the parochial ministry rests upon definite theological foundations, which are carefully related to practice, and are directed to the service of his flock. This indicates a professional view of the ministry.

In their attempts to define the idea of a profession, sociologists and historians have suggested a range of criteria. The more important of these may be summarised by stating that a profession is a form of service which entails the trained exercise of certain skills based upon the application of a recognized body of knowledge. As we have seen, the clergy of the early seventeenth century were called upon to exercise a wide range of skills for the benefit of their parishioners — preaching, teaching and spiritual guidance among others — and these skills were based upon an accepted body of theological knowledge in which the clergy were expected to have acquired a fair degree of expertise.[8]

At the Reformation the traditional idea of priesthood was retained in the Anglican ordinal. Yet at the same time steps were taken to ensure that the clergy should not again become a separate sacerdotal caste. They were educated with their peers and allowed to marry and raise a family. The celebration of the eucharist remained central to the Anglican priest's life and work, but it was no longer his sole occupation. By 1630 the clergy of the Church of England constituted an occupational profession exercising a broad range of functions which were defined in the Ordinal and Prayer Book and given a classical exposition in George Herbert's account of his pastoral ideals.

II

During the course of the eighteenth century the clergy prospered, due to a rise in agricultural rents and land values, and many came to identify themselves with the gentry and their way of life. On Sundays they preached at Morning Prayer and Ante-Communion, and said Evening Prayer in the afternoon. In between they squeezed baptisms, churchings, weddings and burials. Their sermons were often too learned or too dull to hold the attention of the ordinary parishioner. It was no wonder that those who could escape the eye of the squire or parson preferred to sit under the homelier and livelier discourses of Methodist preachers. Parsons rarely celebrated Holy Communion more than three or four times a year and often neglected systematic catechizing or pastoral work.

As a consequence of these developments, many clergymen found themselves free most of the week and financially able to engage in the social pursuits of the gentry. They were also able to undertake the functions attached to the status of a gentleman, such as acting as magistrates.

The early nineteenth century witnessed a gradual return to a more professional view of the priest's life and work. The Evangelical and Tractarian movements promoted higher ideals of Christian discipleship and of clerical vocation. The followers of both movements revived the ideal of the ministry as a sacred calling which required the clergy to separate themselves from worldly affairs and to concentrate exclusively on spiritual matters.[9]

There was a growing tendency in early Victorian society to define each calling's duties more precisely and to demand a more conscientious performance of those duties. As the century advanced, old professions revived and new ones came into being. Doctors, judges, administrators, teachers, social workers, scientists, engineers — all set out to define their distinctive functions and to stake claims for professional status. They also took over work from the clergy: in the school, on the magistrate's bench and in the homes of the poor. By the 1870s the clergy had lost or relinquished many of their secular duties. This enabled them to concentrate upon their distinctively religious functions. In the period between 1750 and 1875, the clergy gradually gave up their secular roles in order to concentrate on their 'charter' roles as defined in the ordinal: preaching, catechizing, leading worship, celebrating the sacraments and pastoral care. Russell interprets this development as partly at least an imitation of the professionalism of the new occupations of the time. Rosemary O'Day argues convincingly that it was a revival of an earlier clerical professionalism, which, as has already been argued, had begun to develop two centuries earlier. Far from the clergy imitating the new professions they, together with the lawyers, provided a model for the new aspirants to professional status.[10]

George Herbert's *The Country Parson* continued to provide a model for Anglican parsons well into the nineteenth century. It was reissued at the beginning of the period by the Clarendon Press, bound together with seven other leading pastoral handbooks in a composite volume called *The Clerical Instructor*, which was reprinted many times. The new pastoral handbooks of the period continued to reflect George Herbert's influence, although their authors attempted to adapt his advice to a rapidly changing society. One of the earliest of these new pastoral handbooks was Edward Monro's *Parochial Work*, which was first published in 1850 when its author was parish priest of a then rural Harrow Weald.[11]

John Keble hailed *Parochial Work* as 'our modern Country Parson'.[12] He valued it chiefly as an expression of the sacramentalism of the Oxford Movement, arguing that the pastoral system it advocated would strike deeper roots than one which relied upon preaching alone. Monro's ideal was based upon the Book of Common Prayer and the Tractarian principle of priestly sacramental mediation. T.T. Carter explains this principle succinctly. The priest's sacramental functions are primary, he argues, because the sacraments are the sole means of grace: the purposes of preaching and teaching, on the other hand, are to make men and women hunger for sacramental grace and to turn them into informed and devout communicants.[13]

Monro, like Newman in the first of the *Tracts for the Times*, calls upon the clergy to rise to a higher sense of professional duty. It is largely their fault that the rural poor are ignorant of the faith, immoral and slack in their religious duties. The clergy must develop a deeper sense of vocation and be willing to work at least as hard as their most hardworking parishioners.

Monro finds the parson's functions to be defined clearly in the Book of Common Prayer: the priest is a leader of worship, celebrant of sacraments, spiritual guide and teacher of the faith. Like the pastoral reformers of two centuries earlier, he argues that, while the priest's sacramental functions are at the heart of his work, the poor must be instructed in the meaning and use of the sacraments if they are to participate fully in their benefits.

A parson's primary task is to establish the regular celebration of Holy Communion each Sunday and holy day. At the same time — here Monro echoes Herbert — he must revive the public recitation of Morning and Evening Prayer. One important test of the reality of a priest's commitment to the poor is his willingness to rise early and turn out late at times when his labourers are able to attend the daily offices. Monro praises Evangelical preachers for arousing the poor to a sense of spiritual need at a time when there was 'a deep lack of religion'. They erred, however, in exaggerating the importance of the sermon. Yet, although it is not a channel of grace in the same way as the sacraments are, the pulpit remains a vital way of awakening a longing for sacramental grace.

In addition to preaching there are two other vital means of popular instruction which parsons must use to arouse the poor from their spiritual torpor to a sense of spiritual need. One is regular pastoral guidance at the parsonage, and the other is the fullest possible use of catechizing. The pastoral guidance of individuals is to be regarded as the parson's 'foremost work'. By 1850 it was already being said that a visiting parson produced a church-going parish. Like Martin Thornton a century later, Monro is sceptical about this claim.[14] It is of course the parson's duty to visit the sick and dying in their homes, but general visiting is too easily time wasted on mere social chat. It is much more fruitful of spiritual results to persuade parishioners to visit the rectory or vicarage for regular spiritual counsel.

Yet, vital as this work is, it does not hold the same promise as catechetical work with children. The characters and habits of adults are already formed and little open to change; children are much more malleable and amenable to indoctrination and spiritual formation. It is every parson's duty not only to teach the Catechism in church on Sunday afternoons, but also to extend its use to weekdays in the elementary schools that are springing up everywhere. These schools are the site of a life and death struggle between two opposed ideals of education: that of the teacher who stresses intellectual instruction, and that of the priest who upholds the primacy of moral and religious training. The future of the church and of the nation rests upon the outcome of this battle. The liberal stress on intellectual education endangers the Christian faith. The training of intellects must be subordinate to training in the spiritual life.

Although two centuries separate Herbert from Monro, and they have their theological differences, there is much they have in common in their visions of the parson's life and work. The parson is responsible for the welfare of his parishioners in every aspect of their lives, secular as well as religious. The overall task is to build up a worshipping community based upon the provisions of the Book of Common Prayer. In the rural parishes about which Herbert and Monro wrote, the parson was usually the only professional person. Nevertheless by the middle of the nineteenth century when Monro's pastoral handbook was published, fundamental changes in society were already taking place.

III

This outline of developments in the Anglican ordained ministry down to the Victorian era has highlighted the rise of a clerical profession charged with an extensive range of tasks. In this last section it will be argued that, despite the straitened circumstances of the modern Church, professional ministers are still needed, and their most valuable contribution is their theologically informed oversight of the local church communities. There are, however, a number of objections to this view.

It might be argued that this account of the development of the ordained ministry is of little more than historical interest, and that English society has changed so fundamentally over the past two centuries that a pastoral tradition rooted in a rural past is of no relevance to a modern industrial society. The parsons about whom Herbert and Monro wrote lived and worked at the heart of the parishes they served; they touched upon all aspects of their parishioners' lives, secular as well as religious; and their teaching supplied the moral and spiritual basis of the social order. Today priests have been banished to the margins of society; they have lost many of their traditional functions to doctors, teachers, social workers, counsellors and a host of other new professions, and even those functions left to them, such as the leadership of worship and preaching, seem of little or no relevance to the great mass of people who never enter a church door. Finally, it is clear that the clergy can no longer hope to be called upon to meet the moral and spiritual needs of more than one section of an increasingly pluralist society.

It might also be argued that the priesthood scarcely qualifies as a profession in a society dominated by scientific and technological values. Modern professions require their recruits to acquire a publicly recognised body of knowledge and a mastery of a range of technical skills. Theology appears to many to be like the spells of the 'wise woman' of folk-lore; and the parson's skills seem as obsolete as those of the charcoal-burner.

Also, in the past, a clergyman could command respect because of his status as a gentleman or because of the authority granted to him by the rite of ordination to the sacred ministry. Today such claims count for little. In modern society we are judged on the basis of our competence.[15] Consequently priests can gain a hearing only if they can command at least the respect if not the assent of sceptical and secular minds. They have therefore to be competent as theologians and able to expound their traditional faith in ways that make sense in a non-traditional culture. Only then will the clergy be able to dispel the suspicion that they are outmoded as a profession.

Others contend that professionalism is incompatible with Christian ministry. Professionals, it is claimed, lord it over passive clients, contrary to Christian ideals of community and service. That this kind of authoritarianism has disfigured church life cannot be denied. John Whale, for example, concludes his history of Barnes parish church and its incumbents by highlighting 'two propensities which our story discloses: obscurantism and authoritarianism'.

> The incumbent who folds his arms and declares that by virtue of his ordination he knows best — and he is still a familiar figure — is in retreat from reason . . . stripped of the status conferred on him by comparative affluence, the incumbent claims instead the mysterious superiority of the priest. He does himself and his profession a disservice. In an age when authority has to be earned, the claim is troubling to the onlooker. He sees incumbents who cannot carry the part they have themselves chosen. They are imprisoned in loneliness by the barriers it sets between them and other people; believing that anything they choose to do is directed by a higher power, they are corrupted into doing nothing; they are depressed to the verge of insanity by the gap between their expectations from their special magic and its barely perceptible achievements.[16]

Such distortions of the ideal of clerical professionalism are still to be found. Some priests seem to believe the grace of ordination raises them above ordinary rational or human considerations. If we are to avoid such deviations it is important to bear in mind that the clergy do not belong to a superior caste set above inferior clients, and are not possessed of a higher wisdom. The clergy and laity alike belong to one priestly body, in which the rôle of the clergy is to contribute to the work of the body as a whole.

The kind of clerical professionalism that John Whale found in the history of one parish church and its incumbents has often surfaced in the history of the Church in authoritarianism and twisted appeals to sacerdotal powers. John Oman has written:

> Unfortunately an official religious relation is much easier to cultivate than a human. But the main hindrance is not the dog-collar on the neck, but what has been called the dog-collary mind, which would only shout 'parson' at you the more loudly for being dressed in a kilt and a pink tie. Anyone who takes his calling seriously seldom escapes the marks of it, and, within due limits, there is no reason why he should. But there is a great difference in the kind of professional parson he is taken to be, whether one who, as Seeley described him, regards God as the head of the clerical profession, or one who in all his ways plainly shows that he regards God as the Father of all men.[17]

It is clear that in this passage Oman, like Whale, is not attacking the idea of a professional parson, but its perversion in the clericalism which has too often disfigured the face of the Church.

Having attempted to defend the ideal of a professional ministry against its detractors, it remains to describe that ideal in a little more detail. The essential idea of a professional ministry disclosed by our historical survey, stripped of the accidents of time, is of a body of men and women set apart by the church to study and reflect upon the Christian faith, in order to learn how to interpret and communicate that faith in relation to the needs of the community they serve.

In recent years there has developed a greater awareness of the importance of the local church and of the full range of ministries within it. The Second Vatican Council recognised the importance of all ministries in the Church and highlighted the significance of the local congregation in words that are relevant to Anglicans as well as Roman Catholics. 'The Church of Christ is truly present in all legitimate local congregations . . . local churches, united with their pastors, are themselves called churches in the New Testament . . . in their own locality Christians constitute the new people of God.'[18] The local church consists of all those who have been baptized and who share in Christ's priestly work. They meet

each week to offer the eucharist, to hear God's word, to
encourage one another and to find ways of commending the
Christian message to those outside their fellowship. Nowadays there is a better understanding than in the past that all
have a part to play in the life and work of the local church.
What then is the distinctive form of service that the local
Christian community now requires of the ordained and professional minister?

Today there appears to be a broad measure of ecumenical
agreement about the nature and functions of the ordained
ministry. A recent consultation between Lutherans and Roman Catholics in Germany agreed that 'all Christians participate in Christ's priesthood' and constitute 'a single priestly
people'.[19] In the sixteenth century the Reformers redis-
covered this forgotten truth in the Scriptures and protested
against the unwarranted elevation of the clergy above the
laity. Nevertheless, apart from a minority of radicals, they did
not deny the need for a separate and properly authorised
ordained ministry. Modern Protestants and Catholics are able
to agree that the chief functions of the ordained ministry are
the 'public proclamation of the gospel and the administration
of the sacraments'; and that the ministry is to be exercised
on behalf of all even though it cannot be 'entrusted to all'.
The extent of modern ecumenical agreement is evident too
in the 1982 World Council of Churches statement on Baptism, Eucharist and Ministry.

> Presbyters serve as pastoral ministers of word and sacraments
> in a local eucharistic community. They are preachers and
> teachers of the faith, exercise pastoral care, and bear respon-
> sibility for the discipline of the congregation to the end that
> the world may believe and that the entire membership of the
> Church may be renewed, strengthened and equipped in
> ministry. Presbyters have particular responsibility for the
> preparation of members for Christian life and ministry.[20]

The ordained ministers' tasks, then, include the proclamation of the Word of God; the celebration of the sacraments;
and the encouragement of spiritual growth within their parishioners. To accomplish these tasks adequately the clergy

need to learn various techniques like teaching, public speaking and counselling. But their chief concern is the study of theology. What distinguishes their work from the many other types of teaching and counselling to be found in the modern world is that they are rooted in the Christian Gospel. It may further be argued that the chief task of ordained ministers is to act as theologians to their congregations. In German, as H.H. Farmer has pointed out, the word 'theologian' is particularly associated with the work of the parish minister. The 'most distinctive function' of the minister '(for it is one which no one else in the Christian community can discharge) is to produce, preserve and utilise a sound theology'.[21]

The ordained minister, then, is called to equip members of local congregations for their mission in the world by being their theologian. The Christian faith is not merely a human discovery or achievement or a set of philosophical ideals, but is God's revelation of himself in Jesus Christ. The modern religious world is like a supermarket with an enormous range of spiritual goods on display. The newer and more exotic lines often look more tempting than the old and established ones. It is the task of the local church, and of the ordained minister as theologian and teacher, not to denigrate other faiths, but to show what is distinctive about the Christian faith and why they think it is true. The argument, then, is that what we should expect of professional priests is that they should be competent theologians, who are able to communicate the Gospel.

The kind of theology which seems most relevant to their task has been described as a 'practical theology'. This involves critical thought about God and our relation to him, and attempts to bring the resources of the Christian tradition — Scripture, theology, prayer, worship — to bear upon the needs of daily life. It is the responsibility of ordained ministers to take a lead in such theological exploration and to help their fellow Christians to share a common vision and sense of direction.[22]

Although the clergy have lost much of the authority and status they enjoyed in the past, they remain key figures in the life and work of the local church. Having shed their secular functions, they are free to concentrate on their primary religious tasks. In the future the Church of England is likely to place even greater emphasis than it has done hitherto upon the contributions of lay ministries of various kinds, and of ordained ministers who earn their livings in secular callings. Nevertheless there will be a continuing need for a professional body of ordained ministers charged with the task of being pastors to the pastors and teachers of the teachers.[23]

Notes

1. Rosemary O'Day, 'The Clerical Renaissance in England and Wales', *Religion in Victorian Britain: Volume I, Traditions* ed. Gerald Parsons, (Manchester, 1988), pp. 184–212.
2. Edward P. Echlin, *The Priest as Preacher: Past and Future* (Cork and Dublin, 1973).
3. O'Day, op. cit., pp. 185 f.
4. George Herbert, *The Country Parson, The Temple* ed. John N. Wall, (London, 1981).
5. ibid., pp. 62 ff.
6. See Gene Edward Veith, *Reformed Spirituality: The Religion of George Herbert* (London and Toronto, 1985) for an exposition of *The Country Parson*.
7. Clement F. Rogers, *An Introduction to the Study of Pastoral Theology* (Oxford, 1912), pp. 59 ff.
8. There is a good discussion of the issues in Walter E. Wiest and Elwyn A. Smith, *Ethics in Ministry: A Guide for the Professional* (Minneapolis, 1990), pp. 71–81.
9. See Anthony Russell, *The Clerical Profession* (London, 1980) and Brian Heeney, *A Different Kind of Gentleman* (Connecticut, 1976).
10. O'Day, op. cit., pp. 185 ff.
11. Edward Monro, *Parochial Work* (Oxford, 1850).
12. John Keble, Occasional Papers and Reviews (Oxford, 1877), pp. 371 ff.
13. T.T. Carter, *The Doctrine of the Priesthood in the Church of England* (London, 1958), pp. 270 f.
14. Martin Thornton, *Pastoral Theology: A Reorientation* (London, 1958), pp. 270 f.
15. Paul Avis, *Authority, Leadership and Conflict in the Church* (London, 1992), Chapter 8.

16 John Whale, *One Church, One Lord* (London, 1979), pp. 164 ff.

17. John Oman, *Concerning the Ministry* (London, 1936), p. 25.

18. Dogmatic Constitution on the Church (*Lumen Gentium*), Section 26, *The Documents of Vatican II* ed. W.M. Abbott (New York, 1966), pp. 50 ff.

19. K. Lehmann and W. Pannenberg, eds., *The Condemnations of the Reformation Era. Do they still divide?* (Minneapolis, 1990), pp. 147 ff.

20. World Council of Churches, Faith and Order Paper No. 111, *Baptism, Eucharist and Ministry* (Geneva, 1982), pp. 20 ff.

21. H.H. Farmer, *The Servant of the Word* (London, 1941), p. 10.

22. J.W. De Gruchy, *Theology and Ministry in Context and Crisis* (London 1987), pp. 40 ff.

23. Valuable discussions of the subject of this essay are to be found in the following: G.R. Dunstan, 'The Sacred Ministry as a Learned Profession', *The Sacred Ministry* ed. G.R. Dunstan, (London, 1970), pp. 1–10; M. Thornton, *Essays in Pastoral Reconstruction* (London, 1960), pp. 35–47; M. Thornton, *The Rock and the River* (London, 1965), pp. 131–146; R. Greenwood, *Transforming Priesthood: A New Theology of Mission and Ministry*, (London, 1994).

Afterword

Geoffrey Rowell

Debates about order and ministry have been characteristic of the Church, and particularly of the church in the west, throughout its history. As Jean Daniélou wrote in the third volume of his history of early Christian doctrine, *The Origins of Latin Christianity*, 'The *corpus* or "society" formed by Christian believers is . . . characterised by . . . three features — faith, discipline, hope. But it also has a hierarchical structure, for the preservation of these things is entrusted to those who preside over the assembly, who are the successors of the apostles and to whom Christ has committed the Church.'[1] He points out how Cyprian developed the doctrine of the episcopate in a way that was to have profound influence on the Latin West. The tension between ecclesiastical authority and spiritual power is found in the early Church in the disputes over Montanism, and in the later pure church theories of the Donatists. The same tension is manifest in the disputes between the institutional church and 'prophetic' and 'spiritual' movements in the Middle Ages, and in the stance of the radical Reformation against the mainstream Reformers. In the context of ecumenical discussion questions concerning order and ministry have been prominent. They are prominent again as declining vocations to the ordained ministry and the need to sustain the ministry of the church to the whole nation combine with financial pressures

161

and burgeoning lay ministries to bring powerful pressures to bear on older understandings of the order and ministry of the Church. A wise discernment is needed to disentangle what belongs to the inheritance of a dated and distorting clerical-ism, and what belongs to the apostolic order and pattern of the Church.

No human community can exist without structures, and the Church is no exception to this. Yet the Church does not merely reflect an old order but points forward to the new. Its order is one of ministry — as F.D. Maurice wrote in the mid-nineteenth century, 'the whole sacerdotal caste in Christen-dom has the name of 'ministers' or 'servants'. From the Bishop of Rome down to the founder of the last new sect in the United States of America, everyone who deals with the gospel at all, or pretends in any sense to have a divine commission, assumes this name as the description of his office.'[2] The order of the Church derives from one who said that he was amongst us as one who served. The ambiguities of power continually challenge those who exercise leadership and authority in the Church.

But although ministry is a primary category, as exercised in the Church it means more than a general ethical respon-sibility: it has as its primary character a specific action under-taken on behalf of God and his Church. Ministry belongs to the being and identity of the Church, for the Church's mission and ministry is a continuation of the mission and ministry of Christ. '*As* the Father sent me, *so* am I sending you.' (John 20: 21) The mission and ministry of the people of God as a whole spring from their baptism into the death and resurrection of the Lord, and their participation in the power of his life-giving Spirit, who binds the Church in unity, enables it to grow in holiness, and impels it into the world in mission.

As grace perfects and transforms nature and does not destroy it, so the community of the new creation is not an undifferentiated whole. 'There is a variety of gifts but always the same Spirit; there are all sorts of service to be done, but always to the same Lord' (1 Corinthians 12: 4–5). 'And to some, his gift was that they should be apostles, to some prophets, to some, evangelists, to some pastors and teachers; so that the saints together make a unity in the work of service, building up the body of Christ' (Ephesians 4: 11–12). The diversity is to serve the unity: the unity is manifested in a rich diversity. Yet even that diversity, although equal in purpose and in the embodiment of a single Christlike calling and identity, is expressed in an order in which it is possible to say that in the Church the apostles are placed first, and are also the foundation. And their ministry of mission and oversight is continued and maintained in the ministry of oversight, the *episcopē*, exercised by the bishops whose task it is to enable the ministry of the whole people of God. In the Pastoral Epistles Timothy is commanded to 'fan into flame' the gift bestowed by the laying-on of hands, and to 'keep the pattern of sound teaching'. 'You have been trusted to look after something precious: guard it with the help of the Holy Spirit who lives in us' (2 Timothy 1: 6, 13–14).

The Spirit who animates and shapes the Christian community is the Spirit who catches us into the *koinonia*, the belonging-togetherness of the Trinity. The very life of God has an order of giving and receiving, a *perichoresis* (the original word meant 'a round dance') in which there is a mutual indwelling in love. Within that order there is a co-equality, and yet also an order and hierarchy. As the Cappadocian Fathers recognised, it is the Father who is the *archē* (the beginning) and *pēgē* (the fountain source) of God-head, whose *principatus* is found in a self-giving, an outpouring of being in the eternal generation of the Son, through whom the Spirit is poured upon the Church, that the Church may be fashioned in the likeness of Christ, and in that true filiation may be brought to the heart of the Father's creative love. In the Trinity reciprocity and hierarchy meet. It is the Trinity which is the Divine order, and the Divine life which is the constraining love shaping the order and ministry of the Church. Christ, who is Lord and Master, is the one who deacons, both as servant and emissary: the great High Priest whose priestly prayer of sacrifice is made on the altar of the cross. The priesthood of the whole people of God, and the ministerial priesthood which represents that priesthood to the Church, and does so by a call to share in a particular way in the intercessory priesthood of Christ, is patterned on that sacrifice. In the celebration of the eucharist both those who preside and those who pray with them are 'drawn into the movement of' Christ's 'self-offering'. There they become the Church, for as the Church makes the eucharist so the eucharist makes the Church. 'Behold the mystery of yourselves, be what you receive, receive what you are.' (St Augustine)

The distortions of hierarchy, and the distortions of an egalitarian collectivism, and the distortions of an atomistic individualism, as they are manifested in the life of the church of this or any age, are judged by the being in communion of God as Trinity, in whose light we see light. It is in that light that historical re-assessments of the origin and development of the ordained ministry are to be seen, and that contemporary explorations of the theology of the laity and the lay ministries and more corporate styles of ministry are to be judged. In an essay on 'The Problem of Order in Early Christianity and the Ancient Church' Hans von Campenhausen issued a timely reminder that just as 'no Church lives by the continuity and ecumenical solidarity of its order', neither 'does it live by discontinuity and the capriciousness of perpetual change'. 'It is of the essence of order . . . that it should be, as far as possible, uniform, coherent, and intended to last, that though its form may change, it must be continually borne with, upheld and preserved, provided that order does not become of greater moment than the spirit, so that it can serve the uninhibited preaching of Christ, and the bringing of his forgiveness, without impeding it in any way whatsoever.'[3] These essays, grounded in a Trinitarian ecclesiology, challenge us to a renewed exploration of an understanding of order and ministry rooted in the preaching of the apostolic faith, and serving and enabling the unity which the Spirit gives.

Notes

1. J. Daniélou, *The Origins of Latin Christianity*, ET, 1977, pp. 432–3.
2. F.D. Maurice, *The Kingdom of Christ*, 1891, II, p. 109.
3. H. von Campenhausen, *Tradition and Life in the Church*, ET, 1968, pp. 132–3.

Oct 86
145 last weeks